Stories for a Woman's Heart

THE SECOND COLLECTION

Stories for a Woman's Heart

THE SECOND COLLECTION

Over 100 More Stories to Delight Her Soul

COMPILED BY ALICE GRAY

WITH JUDY GORDON AND NANCY JO SULLIVAN

Multnomah®Publishers *Sisters, Oregon*

STORIES FOR A WOMAN'S HEART: THE SECOND COLLECTION
published by Multnomah Publishers, Inc.

International Standard Book Number: 1-57673-859-0

Cover image by Corbis
Background cover image by Photodisc
Interior illustrations by Digital Stock

Unless otherwise indicated, Scripture quotations are taken from:
The Holy Bible, New International Version © 1973, 1984 by International Bible
Society, used by permission of Zondervan Publishing House

The Living Bible (TLB) © 1971. Used by permission of
Tyndale House Publishers, Inc. All rights reserved.

Also quoted: The Holy Bible, King James Version (KJV)

Multnomah is a trademark of Multnomah Publishers, Inc.
and is registered in the U.S. Patent and Trademark Office.
The colophon is a trademark of Multnomah Publishers, Inc.

Stories for the Heart is a trademark of Multnomah Publishers, Inc.
and is registered in the U.S. Patent and Trademark Office.

For information:
MULTNOMAH PUBLISHERS, INC. • P.O. BOX 1720 • SISTERS, OR 97759

Library of Congress Cataloging-in-Publication Data:

Stories for a woman's heart: over 100 stories to encourage her soul/
compiled by Alice Gray, Judy Gordon, and Nancy Jo Sullivan. p.cm.
ISBN: 1-57673-474-9 (alk. Paper)
    1-57673-859-0
    1. Christian women–Religious life–Anecdotes. 2. Christian women—conduct of
life–Anecdotes. I. Gray, Alice, 1939– II. Gordon, Judy, 1952– III. Sullivan, Nancy
Jo, 1956–
    BV4527.S735 1999   98-52834
    248.8'43–dc21   CIP

01 02 03 04 05 06 07—10 9 8 7 6 5 4 3 2 1

To dear friends

who have left their imprint on our hearts…

Thank you,

Alice, Judy, and Nancy

A SPECIAL THANK-YOU TO...

Jennifer Gates
There would be no beginning, middle,
or end of this book without you.

The authors who wrote wonderful stories
This isn't our book...it's yours.

*Doreen Button, Casandra Lindell,
Erika Poston, and Lenette Stroebel*
You helped us find and choose extraordinary stories.

*Linda Ho-Honshelt, Sarah McGhehey,
and Julee Schwarzburg*
Only the Lord could keep an account of
all the ways you helped.

Alice Gray
You are the queen of stories, the collector of treasured tales.
Your heart is the crown jewel of this series.
We love and appreciate you.
Judy and Nancy

Al Gray
Your tender care has never disappointed.
Alice

Our heavenly Father
You guided, encouraged, provided, delighted,
and sheltered us in the shadow of Your wings.

Compassion

Treasured Moments

Inspiration

True Love

Faith

Compassion

MENDED

Touched by a loving heart,
Wakened by kindness,
Chords that were broken
Will vibrate once more.

FANNY CROSBY

ONE GLASS OF MILK

AUTHOR UNKNOWN

One day a poor boy who was selling goods from door to door to pay his way through school, found he had only one thin dime left, and he was hungry.

He decided he would ask for a meal at the next house. However, he lost his nerve when a lovely young woman opened the door. Instead of a meal he asked for a drink of water. She thought he looked hungry so brought him a large glass of milk. He drank it slowly and then asked, "How much do I owe you?"

"You don't owe me anything," she replied. "Mother has taught us never to accept pay for a kindness."

He said, "Then I thank you from my heart."

As Howard Kelly left that house, he not only felt stronger physically, but his faith in God and man was strong also. He had been ready to give up and quit.

Years later that young woman became critically ill. The local doctors were baffled. They finally sent her to the big city, where they called in specialists to study her disease. Dr. Howard Kelly was called in for the consultation. When he heard the name of the town she came from, a strange light filled his eyes. Immediately he rose and went down the hall of the hospital to her room. Dressed in his doctor's gown, he went in to see her. She didn't remember him, but he recognized her at once. He went back to the consultation room, determined to do his best to save her life. From that day on he gave special attention to the case.

After a long struggle, the battle was won. Dr. Kelly requested the business office to pass the final bill to him for approval. He looked at it, then wrote something on the edge, and the bill was sent to her room. She feared to open it, for she was sure it would take the rest of her life to pay for it all. Finally she looked, and something caught her attention on the side of the bill. She read these words: *Paid in full with one glass of milk. Dr. Howard Kelly*

Those who are happiest
are those who do the most for others.

BOOKER T. WASHINGTON

DON'T LET IT END THIS WAY

Sue Monk Kidd

he hospital was unusually quiet that bleak January
evening, quiet and still, like the air before a storm. I
stood in the nurses' station on the seventh floor and glanced at the clock.
It was 9:00 P.M.

I threw a stethoscope around my neck and headed for Room 712, the
last room on the hall. Room 712 had a new patient, Mr. Williams: a man
all alone, a man strangely silent about his family.

As I entered the room, Mr. Williams looked up eagerly, but dropped
his eyes when it was only me, his nurse. I pressed the stethoscope over his
chest and listened. Strong, slow, even beating. Just what I wanted to hear.
Very little indicated that he had suffered a slight heart attack a few hours
earlier.

He looked up from his starched bed. "Nurse, would you…" He hesitated, tears filling his eyes. Once before he had started to ask me a question but had changed his mind.

I touched his hand, waiting.

He brushed away a tear. "Would you call my daughter? Tell her I've
had a heart attack. A slight one. You see, I live alone and she is the only

family I have." His respiration suddenly speeded up.

I turned his nasal oxygen up to eight liters a minute. "Of course, I'll call her," I said, studying his face.

He gripped the sheets and pulled himself forward, his face tense with urgency. "Will you call her right away—as soon as you can?" He was breathing fast—too fast.

"I'll call her first thing," I said, patting his shoulder. "Now you get some rest."

I flipped off the light. He closed his eyes—such young blue eyes in his fifty-year-old face.

Room 712 was dark except for a faint night-light under the sink. Oxygen gurgled in the green tubes above his bed. Reluctant to leave, I moved through the shadowy silence to the window. The panes were cold. A foggy mist curled through the hospital parking lot. Above, snow clouds quilted the night sky. I shivered.

"Nurse," he called. "Could you get me a pencil and paper?"

I dug a scrap of yellow paper and a pen from my pocket and set them on the bedside table.

"Thank you," he said. I smiled and left.

I walked back to the nurses' station and sat in a squeaky swivel chair by the phone. Mr. Williams's daughter was listed on his chart as the next of kin. I got her number from information and dialed. Her soft voice answered.

"Janie, this is Sue Kidd, a registered nurse at the hospital. I'm calling about your father. He was admitted today with a slight heart attack and…"

"No!" she screamed into the phone, startling me. "He's not dying is he?" It was more of a painful plea than a question.

"His condition is stable at the moment," I said, trying hard to sound convincing.

Silence. I bit my lip.

"You must not let him die!" she said. Her voice was so utterly compelling that my hand trembled on the phone.

"He is getting the very best care," I said.

"But you don't understand," she pleaded. "My daddy and I haven't spoken in almost a year. We had a terrible argument on my twenty-first birthday, over my boyfriend. I ran out of the house. I…I haven't been back. All these months I've wanted to go to him for forgiveness. The last thing I said to him was, 'I hate you.'"

Her voice cracked and I heard her heave great agonizing sobs. I sat, listening, tears burning my eyes. A father and a daughter, so lost to each other! Then I was thinking of my own father, many miles away. It had been so long since I had told him I loved him.

As Janie struggled to control her tears, I breathed a prayer: *Please, God, let this daughter find forgiveness.*

"I'm coming now! I'll be there in thirty minutes," she said. *Click.* She had hung up.

I tried to busy myself with a stack of charts on the desk. I couldn't concentrate. Room 712. I knew I had to get back to 712. I hurried down the hall nearly in a run. I opened the door.

Mr. Williams lay unmoving. I reached for his pulse. There was none.

"Code ninety-nine. Room 712. Code ninety-nine. Stat." The alert was shooting through the hospital within seconds after I called the switchboard through the intercom by the bed. Mr. Williams had had a cardiac arrest.

With lightning speed I leveled the bed and bent over his mouth, breathing air into his lungs. I positioned my head over his chest and compressed. One, two, three. I tried to count. At fifteen, I moved back to his mouth and breathed as deeply as I could. Where was help? Again I compressed and breathed. Compressed and breathed. He could not die!

Oh, God. I prayed. *His daughter is coming. Don't let it end this way.*

The door burst open. Doctors and nurses poured into the room, pushing emergency equipment. A doctor took over the manual compression of the heart. A tube was inserted through his mouth as an airway. Nurses plunged syringes of medicine into the intravenous tubing.

I connected the heart monitor. Nothing. Not a beat. My own heart pounded. "God, don't let it end like this. Not in bitterness and hatred. His daughter is coming. Let her find peace."

"Stand back," cried a doctor. I handed him the paddles for the electrical shock to the heart. He placed them on Mr. Williams's chest. Over and over we tried. But nothing. Mr. Williams was dead.

A nurse unplugged the oxygen. The gurgling stopped. One by one they left, grim and silent.

How could this happen? How? I stood by his bed, stunned. A cold wind rattled the window, pelting the panes with snow. Outside seemed a bed of blackness, cold and dark. How could I face his daughter?

When I left the room, I saw her against the wall by a water fountain. A doctor, who had been in 712 only moments before, stood at her side, talking to her, gripping her elbow. Then he moved on, leaving her slumped against the wall.

Such pathetic hurt reflected from her face. Such wounded eyes. She knew. The doctor had told her that her father was gone.

I took her hand and led her into the nurses' lounge. We sat on little green stools, neither saying a word. She stared straight ahead at a pharmaceutical calendar, glass-faced, looking fragile.

"Janie, I'm so sorry," I said. It was pitifully inadequate.

"I never hated him, you know. I loved him," she said.

God, please help her, I prayed.

Suddenly, she whirled toward me. "I want to see him," she said.

My first thought was, *Why put yourself through more pain? Seeing him will only make it worse.* But I got up and wrapped my arm around her. We walked slowly down the corridor to 712. Outside the door I squeezed her hand, wishing she would change her mind about going inside. She pushed open the door.

We moved to the bed, huddled together. Janie leaned over the bed and buried her face in the sheets.

I tried not to look at her, at this sad, sad good-bye. I backed against the bedside table. My hand fell upon a scrap of yellow paper. I picked it up and I read: *My dearest Janie, I forgive you. I pray you will also forgive me. I know that you love me. I love you, too. Daddy.*

The note was shaking in my hands as I thrust it toward Janie. She read it once. Then twice. Her tormented face grew radiant. Peace began to glisten in her eyes. She hugged the scrap of paper to her breast.

"Thank You, God," I whispered, looking up at the window. A few crystal stars blinked through the blackness. A snowflake hit the window and melted away, gone forever.

Life seemed as fragile as a snowflake on the window. *Thank You, God, that relationships, sometimes as fragile as snowflakes, can be mended.* But there is not a moment to spare.

I crept from the room and hurried to the phone. I would call my own father. I would say, "I love you."

MAY BASKETS

FAITH ANDREWS BEDFORD

*I*t's May Day and the warm sunshine has finally coaxed my gardens into bloom. As my children carefully tuck tiny, spring flowers into the bright paper baskets they will take to our neighbors, they beg me to tell them again the story of the years my sisters and I took May baskets to the witch.

Mrs. Pearson wasn't really a witch, but she lived on our lane in an old gray cottage whose overgrown yard was enclosed by a sagging fence. Her gardens, Mother said, were once the envy of the neighborhood, and her home-baked cookies were the best. Now, we rarely saw her. At Halloween, she would place a bowl of candy on her porch and hide behind her faded curtains. When carolers came to her door at Christmas, her house remained silent and dark. Still every year when my sisters and I made May baskets, Mother would urge us to take one to Mrs. Pearson.

Our other neighbors always made a great fuss, but Mrs. Pearson never opened the door. Year after year, our delicate baskets hung on her doorknob until the daffodils dangled limply and the forsythia turned brown.

The year I turned ten, I begged Mother to let us skip Mrs. Pearson's house. She just quietly shook her head. "You might not think so, but I *know* your baskets bring joy to that lonely old lady." So once again, Ellen and I, holding firmly to Beth's chubby little hand, crept up to Mrs. Pearson's door, knocked rather half-heartedly, and scurried behind a lilac bush. "This is silly," I said to Ellen. "She never comes out."

"Ssshhh," Ellen whispered fiercely, pointing toward the door as it slowly opened. A tiny, white-haired lady stepped onto the porch. She removed the May basket from her doorknob and sat down on the top step, our basket in her lap. Suddenly, she put her face in her hands.

"Oh dear, she's crying!" said Beth, darting out from behind the lilac. Mother had put Beth in our charge, so Ellen and I quickly climbed up the steps after her. We found her gently patting Mrs. Pearson's shoulder.

"Are you all right?" I asked with concern.

"Yes, dear, I'm fine," she said as she looked up, wiping her cheeks. "You don't know how much I love your little May baskets. I always leave them on the door so all the passersby can admire them." She paused and smiled shyly. "I just got a bit overwhelmed at the happy memories. You see, long ago my sister and I used to make May baskets just like these."

Beth kept patting her shoulder.

"Would you girls like to come in for some milk and graham crackers?" Mrs. Pearson asked. "I could show you pictures of when my sister and I were just about your age."

"Yes," declared Beth, marching through the open door. Because Mother had told us not to let Beth out of our sight, Ellen and I followed.

As we sat in Mrs. Pearson's tidy little parlor eating our graham crackers, she showed us old photographs of her and her sister rolling hoops down sunlit hillsides, playing with their dolls in the woods, and, best of all, proudly holding their little paper May baskets trimmed with long ribbons.

I wish I could say that after our visit, Mrs. Pearson began tending her garden again or that she answered the door at Halloween and admired our costumes, but she didn't. Nevertheless, for the next several years—until we got too old to weave paper baskets and hide behind lilac bushes—each May Day, we would climb the steps to her front porch and find a little basket just for us. It was full of cookies cut in the shape of flowers, with pink frosting and sugar sprinkles.

A LITTLE CUP
OF WATER

AUTHOR UNKNOWN

It was one of the hottest days of the dry season. We had not seen rain for almost a month. The crops were dying. Cows had stopped giving milk.

The creeks and streams were long gone back into the earth. It was a dry season that would bankrupt several farmers before it was through. Every day, my husband and his brothers would go about the arduous process of trying to get water to the fields. Lately this process had involved taking a truck to the local water rendering plant and filling it up with water. But severe rationing had cut everyone off. If we didn't see some rain soon, we would lose everything.

It was on this day that I learned the true lesson of sharing and witnessed the only miracle I have seen with my own eyes. I was in the kitchen making lunch for my husband and his brothers when I saw my six-year-old son, Billy, walking toward the woods. He wasn't walking with the usual carefree abandon of a youth but with a serious purpose. I could only see his back. He was obviously walking with a great effort, trying to be as still as possible. Minutes after he disappeared into the woods, he came running out again, toward the house. I went back to making sandwiches, thinking that whatever task he had been doing was completed.

Moments later, however, he was once again walking in that slow purposeful stride toward the woods. This activity went on for an hour: walk carefully to the woods, run back to the house. Finally I couldn't stand it any longer, and I crept out of the house and followed him on his journey (being very careful not to be seen, as he was obviously doing important work and didn't need his mommy checking up on him). He was cupping both hands in front of him as he walked, being very careful not to spill the water he held in them...maybe two or three tablespoons were held in his tiny hands.

I sneaked in close as he went into the woods. Branches and thorns slapped his little face, but he did not try to avoid them. He had a much higher purpose. As I leaned in to spy on him, I saw the most amazing sight.

Several large deer loomed in front of him. Billy walked right up to them. I almost screamed for him to get away. A huge buck with elaborate antlers was dangerously close. But the buck did not threaten him; he didn't even move as Billy knelt down. And I saw a tiny fawn lying on the ground, obviously suffering from dehydration and heat exhaustion, lift its head with great effort to lap up the water cupped in my beautiful boy's hands.

When the water was gone, Billy jumped up to run back to the house, and I hid behind a tree. I followed him back to the house, to a spigot that we had shut off. Billy opened it all the way up and a small trickle began to creep out. He knelt there, letting the drip slowly fill up his makeshift "cup," as the sun beat down on his little back.

And things became clear to me. The trouble he had gotten into for playing with the hose the week before. The lecture he had received about the importance of not wasting water. The reason he didn't ask me to help him. It took almost twenty minutes for the drops to fill his hands.

When he stood up and began the trek back, I was there in front of him. His little eyes just filled with tears. "I'm not wasting," was all he said. As he began his walk, I joined him...with a small pot of water from the kitchen. I let him tend to the fawn. I stayed away. It was his job. I stood on the edge of the woods, watching the most beautiful heart I have ever known working so hard to save another life. As the tears that rolled down my face began to hit the ground, they were suddenly joined by other drops…and more drops…and more. I looked up at the sky. It was as if God, Himself, was weeping with pride.

Some will probably say that this was all just a huge coincidence. That miracles don't really exist. That it was bound to rain sometime. And I can't argue with that…I'm not going to try. All I can say is this: The rain that came that day saved our farm…just like the actions of one little boy saved the life of a fawn.

MRS. AMATULI

NANCI STROUPE

M rs. Amatuli was my teacher in the fourth grade. One day at lunchtime, I was getting ready to eat my same old tuna fish sandwich when Mrs. Amatuli approached me and asked if she could buy my sandwich. She explained that I could use the money to buy a hot lunch from the cafeteria.

I was thrilled. I never bought my lunch from the cafeteria. It was too expensive for my family, and we always carried our lunch and brought the bag back home folded up neatly to use again the next day. My sandwiches were either bologna or tuna fish. It rarely varied beyond that.

You can understand my delight when I had the opportunity to buy a hot lunch. Kids always complained about cafeteria food, but I was very envious of them. It sure looked and smelled good to me.

When we finished lunch that day, Mrs. Amatuli took me aside and said she wanted to explain why she had bought my sandwich. I really didn't care why, but it gave me a few minutes of her precious attention, so I was very quiet as she explained. You see, she was Catholic and she told me that Catholics didn't eat red meat on Fridays—they ate fish on Fridays.

Oh, I couldn't wait to get home and tell my mama that from now on I wanted tuna fish on Fridays. After my mama understood why, she gladly fixed tuna fish for me on Friday. She even fixed it on brown bread because she knew Mrs. Amatuli liked brown bread.

From then on, every Friday I could get in the line with the rest of the kids for a hot lunch. I didn't care how many of the kids complained about cafeteria food. It tasted divine to me!

I realize now that Mrs. Amatuli could have fixed herself a tuna sandwich on Friday. But she bought my sandwich because she saw a little girl who was thrilled over the simple act of having a hot lunch. I will never forget her for her compassion and generosity.

What sunshine is to flowers, smiles are to humanity.
They are but trifles, to be sure,
but scattered along life's pathway,
the good they do is inconceivable.

JOSEPH ADDISON

IVY'S COOKIES

CANDY ABBOTT

The clank of the metal door and the echo of their footsteps rang in the ears of Ivy and Joanne as they walked
down the dingy corridor behind the prison guard toward the "big room."
The aroma of Ivy's homemade chocolate chip cookies wasn't enough to
override the stench of ammonia from the recently mopped floor or the bitterness and anger that hung in the air. Women's Correctional Institute was
not the kind of place where seventeen-year-olds go for an outing, but Ivy
had a mission.

She didn't know what she was getting into, but she had to try. With
trembling fingers, she dialed the number for an appointment at the
prison. Warden Baylor was receptive to Ivy's desire to visit and referred her
to Joanne, another teen who had expressed interest.

"How do we do this?" Ivy asked.

"Who knows? Maybe homemade cookies would break the ice,"
Joanne suggested.

So they baked their cookies and here they were, bearing gifts to
strangers.

"I put almonds in these," Ivy rambled nervously as they moved along.
"The dough was gummier than usual..."

"Don't chatter," the guard snapped. "It gets the prisoners riled."

The harsh words made Ivy jump and her heart pound. She walked the rest of the distance in silence.

"Okay. Here we are," the guard grunted, keys rattling. "You go in. I'll lock the door behind you. Be careful what you say. They have a way of using your words against you. You have fifteen minutes. Holler if you have any trouble."

Ivy noted the prisoners' orange jumpsuits and felt overdressed. *Maybe we shouldn't have worn heels,* she thought. *They probably think we're snobs.*

Remembering the guard's admonition, the girls put the cookies on the table next to plastic cups of juice without a word. Some prisoners leaned against the wall; others stood around—watching. Studying. Thinking. Staring. Nobody talked. Ivy smiled at one of the women, and she scowled back. From then on, she avoided eye contact. After five minutes of strained silence, Joanne whispered, "Let's move away from the table. Maybe they'll come over."

As they stepped back, one of the prisoners blurted out, "I'm gettin' a cookie." The others followed and began helping themselves. Soon they heard the rattle of keys. Time was up.

"What a relief to get outta there," Joanne sighed as a gust of fresh air caressed their perspiring faces.

"Yeah," Ivy agreed. "But there's a tug inside me that says we're not done. Would you be willing to go back?"

Joanne nodded with a half-smile. "How about Thursday after school?"

Week after week they came. And week after week the prisoners ate the cookies, drank the juice, and stood around in silence. Gradually, antagonistic looks were replaced by an occasional smile. Still, Ivy couldn't bring herself to speak—not a word.

Then one Thursday, an evangelist walked in. Her step was sure, her chin was high, and she glowed with the love of God. But she meant business. "I've come to pray with you," she announced. "Let's make a circle."

Ivy was awed by the inmates' compliance. Only a few resisted.

Others, although murmuring, inched their way toward the middle of the room and formed a lopsided circle, looking suspiciously at one another.

"Join hands," the evangelist instructed. "It's not gonna hurt ya, and it'll mean more if you do." Slowly they clasped hands, some grasping hard, others barely touching. "Now, bow your heads." Except for the orange outfits, it could have been a church meeting.

"Okay. We're gonna pray," she continued, "and prayer is just like talking, only to God. I want to hear you tell the Lord one thing you're thankful for. Just speak it out. Don't hold back."

Ivy's palms were sweaty. *I can't pray out loud, Lord. I can't even talk to these women. Guess I should set an example, but they probably don't even like me—think I'm better than them 'cause of my clothes.*

The words of an inmate jolted her from her thoughts.

"I'm thankful, God, for Miss Ivy bringing us cookies every week."

Another voice compounded the shock, "God, thanks for bringing a black lady to see us, not just Quakers and Presbyterians."

Ivy's eyes brimmed with tears as she heard, "Thank you, God, for these two ladies givin' their time every week even though we can't do nothin' to pay 'em back."

One by one, every inmate in the circle thanked God for Ivy and Joanne. Then Joanne managed to utter a prayer of gratitude for the prisoners' words. But when it came Ivy's turn, she was too choked up to speak. Her eyes burned in humble remorse over how wrong she'd been about these women. She wished she could blow her nose, but the inmates were squeezing her hands so tightly, she resorted to loud sniffles and an occasional drip.

The following week, Ivy and Joanne returned, bright-eyed, to find the prisoners talkative.

"Why do you bring us cookies every week?" a husky voice inquired from the corner of the room. When Ivy explained, she inched a few steps closer. "Can you get me a Bible?" she asked. Others wanted to know more about the Jesus who inspires teenagers to visit prisoners.

A ministry was born from Ivy's cookies. What started as a silent act of kindness and obedience turned into a weekly Bible study at the prison, which eventually grew so big it split into several groups that continue to this day. After Joanne married and moved away, Ivy continued to minister to the inmates alone for years. Eventually, Prison Fellowship picked up the baton.

Ivy is a grandmom now. Her radiance has increased over the years, and she brightens any room she enters. But last Thursday afternoon she indulged herself in a good cry. Curled up on the couch, wrapped in the afghan her daughter had made, she wept. Deep sobs racked her body as she remembered it had been one year since her daughter died of asthma. She ached over the loss and felt, for the first time, the full weight of her words, "The kids can live with me." The baby was asleep in his crib and the two girls were in school when the doorbell rang.

There stood a young woman, probably seventeen, with a plate of homemade cookies.

"Are you Ivy Jones?" she asked.

"Yes," she answered, dabbing her eyes with a wadded tissue.

"These are for you," the girl said as she handed the cookies to her with a shy, sad smile, turning to leave without another word.

"Thank you," Ivy whispered in a daze. The girl was halfway down the sidewalk when Ivy called out, "But why?"

"My grandmother gave me her Bible before she died last week, and her last words were, 'Find Ivy Jones and take her some homemade cookies.'"

As the girl walked away, a wave of precious memories, uncertainties, and younger days flooded Ivy's soul. Swallowing the lump in her throat, she choked back a sob and headed toward the phone. *It's been a long time since I talked with Joanne.*

Keep Me Faithful

He sat there in the corridor
Of the convalescent hospital
Trying desperately
To maneuver his wheelchair.
His bony fingers trembled.
A tattered slipper fell off his foot.
I asked if I might help him.
He nodded, and then began to weep.
For a brief moment I put my arms
Around his sagging shoulders.
Then I wheeled him down the narrow hall
To his small warm room.
He thanked me as best as he could.
Then he added nervously
"I hope somebody someday will help you
Like you just helped me."
Lord, I hope so, too.

RUTH HARMS CALKIN
FROM *TELL ME AGAIN, LORD, I FORGET*

ON A STRETCH OF CALIFORNIA FREEWAY

CAROLYN LIGHTFOOT

In a tiny little neighborhood church, I taught Sunday school to a class of seven- to ten-year-olds. Three sisters in my class, who came from extremely poor circumstances, were excited about the upcoming Easter pageant.

I shared their enthusiasm and without thinking, blurted out, "Is everyone getting a new Easter outfit?" The faces of the three young girls provided the answer. Realizing my terrible mistake, I called them over to me after the class was dismissed.

"Listen, girls," I began cautiously, "would you do me a big favor?" They nodded their heads in unison. "I don't have any little girls, so I was wondering if you would let me sew Easter dresses for you this year?"

They looked surprised, but pleased; the oldest girl, who was the spokesperson for the kids, hesitated before she spoke. "What about our little brother?" My heart melted in the warmth of the big sister's love.

"Don't you worry about a thing," I bribed. "I'll take care of all of you." They started jumping up and down, overjoyed at the thought of new Easter clothes. On the way home, I wondered how I would ever afford to keep my promise. I begged for God's help as only the guilty can.

That month I scrimped on groceries and saved up enough to buy patterns and fabric. After telling my story to the merchant in the fabric store, she allowed me an extra fifteen percent off my purchases. One of my work chums, Blanche, listened as I worried out loud about socks to match the bright yellow fabric. She reached for her purse and handed me forty dollars. "Buy them shoes, too," she beamed. My boss overheard our conversation and forked over twenty dollars for ribbons, baskets, and treats. By now I was boohooing, and they joined me in doing that, too, all of us dabbing at our eyes with tissues from Blanche's Kleenex box.

For the next two weeks, I sewed every evening until the dresses were done. Then I shopped for new clothing for the little boy. Baskets, ribbons, socks, shoes, shirt, and jeans lay on my bed, awaiting the children. Their mother agreed to bring the girls over to my house the evening before Easter Sunday, and we turned my kitchen into a beauty shop—washing hair, setting curls, painting clear polish onto small fingernails, gobbling up popcorn, and giggling. Early Sunday morning they trooped back into my home, ready for me to brush out their hair. Never had I seen such happy, proud kids. The girls stood in a row, combed, curled, and as cute as three spring daffodils, holding beribboned baskets. Little brother grinned nonstop and kept rubbing his hands down the legs of his new jeans.

In my heart, however, was a small pocket of guilt. As happy as I was for their joy, I still regretted my misspoken words. My heart felt no redemption on that Easter morning.

Fifteen years later, I was driving down the freeway on the way to my mom's house. A car pulled up beside me, honked, and the driver motioned for me to pull over. Assuming I had a flat tire, I immediately complied. She rolled to a stop behind me, jumped out of the car, ran to the window, frantically motioning for me to roll down the window. She was very excited about something. I was mystified.

"Are you Carolyn? You know, from the little church?" Dumbstruck, I nodded my head. "Oh, I thought it was you. I'm Jackie Wilkins," she bubbled. Her words poured out in a steady stream. "I've never forgotten you. Remember the yellow dresses you made us? We still talk about them. It was our best Easter as kids!"

I got out of the car, met her at the rear bumper, and almost never quit hugging her. That day my guilty heart found redemption on a stretch of California freeway.

Happy are the kind and merciful,
for they shall be shown mercy.

MATTHEW 5:7
THE LIVING BIBLE

MORE THAN A HERO

JAN NATIONS

*S*he was a compliant child. Her bobbed, blond hair, blue eyes, and sweet smile were perfect touches for her likeable seven-year-old personality.

As she waited for the school bus that December morning in 1941, she carried a small, brightly wrapped gift. Glancing at it, she reflected on what was inside. Had she made the right choice?

Her four-mile trip to the small Fredericktown, Missouri, dime store had been both agony and ecstasy. It was such a treat to have money to spend, especially a whole quarter. Even to her father, quarters were scarce. The grueling work in a lead mine yielded too few dollars to support the family and have anything left over. He did painting and wallpapering jobs occasionally, to help people out when they needed him, but the bit of extra income didn't hurt either. Somehow he still found time to do the many fix-up jobs around the small farm, as well. The Depression had brought tougher times than most families had ever seen, and now with war breaking out on December 7, everyone seemed to be reeling from the effects of it all.

But just for that short time in the Ben Franklin ten-cent store, Joan was lost in the wonder. She carefully perused every aisle...wanting to select the one item that would mean the most to the little girl who was going to open it. Her small fingers delicately touched a bottle of perfume. She knew it must be exquisite to cost a whole quarter. But she passed it by and next lingered over a necklace that was the most beautiful one she had ever seen. But it was only twenty cents, and the teacher's instructions had been specific—each student's gift should cost a quarter. Finally, she saw it. Her gaze fell upon an incredible ginger-colored glass dish, which held a box of scented bath powder. The lid was adorned with a Bambi-like deer, and she knew the moment she saw it that it was to be her purchase.

How excited she'd been since then, waiting for the day when it would finally be time to take it to school with her for the Christmas gift exchange.

And now the day was here! The horrible thought occurred to her that it could get broken on the way to school. Why, oh why, had she chosen something breakable? Just then, the big yellow school bus came roaring down the dirt road, and she climbed aboard with a little help from her older sister, Virginia, who would graduate from high school the next year.

No one thought it strange that the same bus carried students ranging from ages six through eighteen. In fact, Joan was made to feel like one of the crowd—not only by Virginia, but by her friends as well. Virginia had a unique talent for making her younger sisters feel so grown up, and it never occurred to her not to want them around. It was quite a relationship the two of them had—more like best friends than older/younger sisters.

Virginia and her friends bade Joan farewell as she joined her classmates in a room shared by four grades at Mine La Motte School.

Little did she know that this would be a day she would remember the rest of her life.

After the usual exercises of learning, the big moment arrived. Joan could hardly wait to see the look on the face of the girl who would open the gift she had so carefully chosen. One by one, the children's names were called to come up and receive their special gift. Watching the girl's eyes light up and huge smile break out was enough for Joan to know her choice had been well made. She was so glad she hadn't picked the perfume or the necklace!

As the pile of gifts began getting small, Joan wondered when her name might be called. But when the last gift had been distributed and no packages remained, her name had still not been called. She was confused, and later the teacher said something to her privately about a family with many children not being able to bring a gift.

Whatever the reason for her being the only one who didn't get a gift, she knew one thing for sure: She was not going to cry. After all, she told herself, Christmas is not about receiving. It's about the gift of all gifts—the birth of the Baby Jesus. And that gift was for her, too.

But it did feel a little strange to be the only person getting on the bus after school who wasn't carrying a Christmas present. She hoped no one would notice.

But she had no sooner sat down by her red-haired sister than Virginia's best friend, Nina Denton, said, "How did your classmate like the gift you brought?"

Joan was glad to be able to say that she had loved it, and hoped the conversation would end there. She didn't want her sister's friends to think there was something wrong with her, that she'd been the only one who didn't receive a gift. But no such luck!

Nina's handsome male friend, Don Anthony, looked her straight in the eye and said, "Joan, show us the gift you got."

Her lower lip quivered ever so slightly, and she prayed no one noticed it as she said, "I didn't get a gift." As she looked into Don Anthony's big brown eyes (and even at seven years old she knew his face was extraordinary) she probably learned the true meaning of the word compassion without even realizing it. Without taking his eyes off her soulful little face he reached into his pocket, pulled out the shiniest quarter she had ever seen, and said, "Here, Joan, you can buy anything you want."

She hesitated and looked toward Virginia to see if she should accept this unexpected and most generous gift.

Virginia smiled and said, "It's okay. You can take it."

Nina, Don, and Virginia all looked at each other with smiles, and knew in their hearts it was going to be a wonderful Christmas for all of them.

None of them knew, of course, how few Christmases Don had left. He went to war shortly after that and returned three years later in a flag-draped casket.

Don Anthony gave two gifts. The one for his country would be the last one he would ever give. But the one to the little girl named Joan is still remembered fifty-four years later.

There is a loftier ambition than merely to stand high in the world.
It is to stoop down and lift those around us a little higher.

HENRY VAN DYKE

THE POWER
OF TOUCH

JILL STEINER

*T*he chatter of young children made the playground feel alive. My job at the daycare was simply to supervise them and make sure no one got hurt or into trouble. I'd hoped this would be easy, but Casey had other ideas. The too-cool-for-his-age, seven-year-old kept running from girl to girl, pushing them and then laughing. Or from boy to boy taking toys. I had already put him in several time-outs, but none of them had changed his behavior. Finally, nerves frazzled, I called for Casey to come to me.

"What, Teacher Jill?" he asked with large, innocent, brown eyes.

Taking a deep breath and praying it would work, I responded, "Casey, if you don't leave the other kids alone, I'm going to make you stand here and hug me."

I thought this would be the worst punishment imaginable for the socially high-ranking second grader, but to my surprise, his face softened. "I wouldn't mind if I had to do that," he said in a soft whisper.

I responded, "Huh?" wondering if I'd heard him correctly.

"I'd like to get some hugs." Casey lowered his eyes to look at the ground. He folded his arms across his stomach. "I don't get many hugs."

Surprised at his words, it took me a second to think of what to say next. "Doesn't your mom give you hugs?"

Casey's chin lowered to the point of almost touching his chest. "My mom says we don't need to hug to show we love each other."

"But does she say she loves you?" I couldn't imagine what it must be like to live without hugs.

"Oh, she tells me she loves me all the time. She just says we aren't huggy people."

"Can I give you a hug?"

As soon as I spoke, Casey lunged at me, his arms wrapping around my waist, squeezing with the force of several unused hugs.

For the rest of the afternoon, Casey glued himself to my side. Every now and then I asked him what he thought about hugs and encouraged him to ask his mom for one when she picked him up that evening.

I watched when his mom arrived after work, and Casey quietly requested a hug. An uncomfortable look washed over her face as she reluctantly nodded and circled her arms around her son. The moment the mother showed her affection through a hug, Casey's face lit up in an unmaskable joy.

The effect of a simple hug on Casey was amazing. A transformation in the seven-year-old's attitude happened right before my eyes. I had always heard how important touch is, but I never fully comprehended the reality of it until I saw the glow it put on Casey's face.

RYAN'S GIFT

NANCY PAULSON

I was busy wrapping packages when a memory from a past Christmas floated through my mind. I tied the ribbon around the package and whispered, "Lord, thank You for memories. What a gift they are."

For years I had taken our three sons and their cousins across town to my grandmother's neighborhood to sing carols and give cookies to four elderly families. My stair-step choir consisted of six boys who were just a year apart in age.

I gathered them together in our kitchen and gave them a crash course on Christmas carols. We baked cookies, ate several, and packaged the rest to give away.

But before we piled into the car, I gave them a pep talk. It went something like this: "You boys are doing a very important work for God. Not too many people remember to take time for dear old folks."

The boys enjoyed this yearly tradition except for Mrs. Coleman's house. She was blind and had lost one leg. Her handicaps frightened them.

As we drove across town, I listened to this discussion. "Who's going to sit on Mrs. Coleman's lap first?"

"Not me," one would retort. "Boy, I don't want to," was a statement bounced about the back seat.

This conversation would end and the following discussion would begin. "Why does she touch our faces?"

"She can't see you, stupid."

"It's yucky. Her hands are cold."

We'd arrived in that old neighborhood and walked from house to house in the order of their popularity. Mrs. Coleman's home was last. Before we entered her house, the boys would fidget and shove to get behind the other. I would ring the doorbell and eventually hear a shaky voice from behind the paint-chipped door calling, "Nancy, is that you? Come in."

The small living room was dark and smelled musty. Mrs. Coleman was always sitting on the far end of her tattered couch. It seemed as if she had not moved since last Christmas. The same dark purple afghan was draped across her lap.

She was always cheerful. I would ask about her health and she would smile and say, "God is good. He seems to take care of all my needs."

However, this particular year was different. Her voice was feeble. She had lost weight, and her frail body slumped deep into the sagging couch.

"Are all the boys here?" she asked. "Yes," I answered, and the boys began their performance.

As the children completed their Christmas carols, Mrs. Coleman leaned forward and threw out her shaking arms. She burst into tears, crying out, "You are my Christmas! You are my Christmas! I wait all year for you children to come see me. You are my whole Christmas."

I will never forget the looks on the boys' faces. Twelve eyeballs bulged, fixed on this poor old woman. They stood breathless. Their bodies were frozen. There wasn't a movement or a sound except Mrs. Coleman's lingering whimpers. Finally, Ryan, the youngest of our group, took two hesitant steps toward her. Then he sprinted across the room and hurled himself into her quivering arms.

Mrs. Coleman's weeping turned to laughter as she squeezed him against her feeble body. She kissed his forehead and touched his face. Her fragile voice trembled, "Oh, Ryan, how much you've grown."

"Yeah, I'm in first grade," Ryan responded. As he slipped out of her arms, he fixed his eyes on the five boys still huddled together in the center of the room. There wasn't a word, but Ryan's stare spoke volumes. Silently, one by one, each boy stepped forward and sat down alongside Mrs. Coleman so she could touch their faces and talk about school and sports.

We had entered a dark, musty room, and for a few brief moments we focused on a lonely old lady. We left the room lightened by God's love that reached out and embraced its sole inhabitant.

Mrs. Coleman went to be with the Lord two months later. But every year as I hear those familiar Christmas carols, I remember the six little voices that sang "We Wish You a Merry Christmas" to an isolated old woman. And I hear Mrs. Coleman saying, "You are my Christmas!"

ROSE-COLORED GLASSES

LIZ HOYT
FROM *RIPPLES OF JOY*

Looking back, I suppose I should have seen it coming. But Beth Ann is a sweet, loving soul. I never suspected she would outsmart me.

I had Beth Ann's best interests at heart. She was always involved in some self-sacrificing service project or another, and I was determined to rescue her from her life of drudgery. I'd convinced her to spend a fun day with me, shopping, visiting, and enjoying lunch. I let her select the day for our outing, the Sunday before Thanksgiving. Perfect for me: I was expecting twelve guests for Thanksgiving, and my lavish dinner plans demanded new table decorations. Spending a day in the city was just what I needed before the hectic holiday season got under way.

Life in the Texas hill country is pretty relaxed, so I didn't think it unusual when Beth Ann suggested we wear jeans and sweatshirts for our shopping spree. Besides, my favorite home-decorating boutique didn't care what I wore as long as I remembered to bring my credit cards.

The Texas sky was clear on the morning of our outing. The Christmas decorations in my little town sparkled in the morning sun, and I hummed "Jingle Bells" as I turned onto the highway for the short drive to Beth Ann's house on the outskirts of San Antonio. Beth Ann is a quiet, gentle spirit with a quick laugh and mischievous, twinkling eyes. She views everyone with a heart of love, and spending time with her always warms me. But that day I was on a mission! Under my expert guidance, Beth Ann would "see the light." She'd finally update her closet and cosmetics. She'd learn to spend more time on herself. After all, she wasn't getting any younger.

She was waiting when I pulled into her drive. We hugged, and she sweetly urged that we continue in her car. I hate riding in her old rattle-trap; she hauls just anybody and anything in it, and it smells like it! My luxury sedan, on the other hand, is comfortable and smells of scented apples.

But you don't argue with a dear soul like Beth Ann, so we were quickly on our way in her smelly and noisy vehicle, laughing, talking, and catching up. I told her about my Thanksgiving plans, my grandson's latest achievements and awards, and the expensive Christmas gifts I planned to buy for my grown children. I entertained her with stories of my busy life in a small town, and in between, in spite of the bumpy ride, I wrote out lists of all the things I needed to purchase that day.

When Beth Ann stopped the car, I absently looked up from my shopping list to see that she had parked among other cars and pickups under a major interstate highway—in what appeared to be an inner-city, asphalt parking lot that sprawled as far as I could see. People of all colors, sizes, and ages were unloading old, beat-up serving tables, card tables, ice chests, and huge coffee urns. They were apparently turning the dirty parking lot into a giant, outdoor dining room.

"Beth Ann, darling—where are we, and what are we doing here?!"

She smiled at me with the tender expression of an angel, handed me a bundle, and said, "Put on this apron, my precious friend. It is time you gave up your rose-colored glasses!"

With that she jumped out of the car, laughed, and put the keys into the pocket of her jeans. I had to run to catch up with her, and we were immediately caught up in the mass of dirty, smelly remnants of humanity milling around, waiting expectantly. The noise from the busy highway far above mingled with the banging and clanging of pots and pans on the dismal parking lot.

Beth Ann waved to one and then another of those filthy beings, calling out greetings and addressing them by name. Leftover dregs of society came up to her to smile and say hello. She talked to each of them. She even—God forbid—*hugged them!*

Then she quietly ordered me to help the people who were setting up the serving area and unloading huge pans of turkey, dressing, sweet potatoes, collard greens, and pumpkin pies. I was furious. My "friend" had tricked me into serving Thanksgiving dinner to bums and losers who wandered homeless and lost on the city streets.

When the food was spread out, the crowd organized itself into orderly lines without fanfare, instruction, or greediness. My hands trembled with disgust and anger as I began to fill plate after plate. The line was endless, and the faceless mass of humanity kept coming.

I don't know when things changed, but slowly I began to see individual faces. Eyes filled with weariness and pain. One by one the hungry filed by. Some stared straight ahead, their eyes blank; some smiled shyly with heads down; some thanked me; many looked at me and said, "God bless you, lady."

Faces became names. Minutes melted into hours, and the names became real people who were afraid, lonely, and hungry. By the time the food was gone, my fear, disgust, and anger had drained away into exhaustion. A sweetness I had not felt in years poured over me, and I found myself smiling, listening, and, yes, even touching.

Beth Ann and I never got to the boutique that day. My mission to rescue and change her was forgotten; instead, I was the one who was changed. I had looked into the faces of weary, hurting people and allowed myself to reach into their hungry souls. I took off my rose-colored glasses and left them lying on that dirty parking lot where real people had shared time, food, and Thanksgiving hope with each other.

Treasured Moments

TEA CUPS AND CURLS

The cups on the creamy lace,
battered hats on tangled curls,
chatter and soft laughter.
My granddaughter and I
are having tea.

JANETTE OKE

SPECIAL OCCASIONS

FAITH ANDREWS BEDFORD

Our friend Steve dropped by to borrow the truck last night just as we were finishing up dinner. My husband poured him a cup of coffee, and he joined us at the table. Steve looked surprised as he sat down. "Do you light candles every night?" he asked. I nodded and smiled.

I remembered that evening so long ago when I called the family to dinner only to have them all stop in astonishment at the dining room door.

"Did I forget an important date?" Bob asked, warily eyeing the flowers and candles on the table.

"Is it somebody's birthday?" queried our son, Drew, as he sat down.

"Mommy, you look so pretty," Sarah said, noticing I'd exchanged my usual jeans for a dress. "Is somebody coming for dinner?"

"Well," I began, trying to voice my feelings, "it's autumn—the air is crisp, the asters are coating the meadow with purple, we're all healthy, and life is good."

The children gave one another their Mom's-gone-round-the-bend-again look and promptly dug into their meat loaf.

How could I explain to them the way I felt after having spent a day helping my friend, Linda, whose mother had died three weeks earlier? After the funeral, I had offered to help her box up everything in her mother's house. I had done the same sad work myself a few years back and knew how comforting it could be to have some company.

We started in the dining room. Linda sighed as she opened a drawer in the sideboard and pulled out a set of linen place mats and matching napkins still in their original box.

"Mother bought these when she and Dad went to Ireland fifteen years ago," she said, running her fingers over the embroidery. "She never used them—said they were for a special occasion."

When we opened the corner cupboard, Linda took down a set of crystal champagne flutes.

"She never used these, either," she said. "She bought them in Chicago and declared that we'd all get to toast Dad and her on their fiftieth wedding anniversary. But then Dad died shortly after their forty-eighth."

With her finger she pinged the rim of one of the flutes, and we both listened to the clear tone. "They could have spent all those years drinking champagne together out of these lovely glasses instead of waiting for a day that would never be shared."

From her mother's closet upstairs, Linda pulled out a blue silk dress with rhinestone buttons. The price tag was still attached.

"Let me guess," I said. "For another special occasion?"

Linda nodded sadly.

When I returned home that day, I caught up on some paperwork. My sister's birthday was in a few days, so I reached into the desk drawer where I keep greeting cards that I buy whenever I see a particularly appropriate one. As I leafed through them, I came across one that said, "For the World's Most Wonderful Mother." I never had a chance to send it, but I still can't bring myself to throw it away.

That night, as I looked at my family around the table, I realized how much I had been taking the future for granted. "Someday we'll…" is often heard at our house. But what if I knew just how many "somedays" were left for me? How would I live my life?

Well, for starters, I decided, I would clean house less and play with the children more. I'd read a book rather than finish some project that I thought was so important. I'd take more walks and more vacations—ride my bike and play the recorder. I'd polish my French instead of the silver.

I'd bear in mind that "perfect" is the enemy of "good enough." I'd watch more sunrises. I'd call old friends I had not spoken to in months and write to my sisters more often. I'd use perfume every day. And I'd always light candles at the dinner table.

My thoughts were interrupted by Eleanor's asking, "Are you going to get dressed up every night now?"

"I just might," I replied.

"So can I wear my pink dress tomorrow night?" she asked, eyes wide with excitement.

I started to say that her pink dress was just for parties and church. I thought of all that extra ironing. Then I caught myself and answered, "Of course you can."

"I think we should make a toast," my husband declared, raising his water goblet. The children giggled and lifted their glasses of milk high.

"To life. To being together. To special occasions," Bob said, meeting my eyes knowingly.

"I'll drink to that," I said, clinking my glass with everyone's in turn. "May they happen often."

And they have.

THE RED CARPET

LINDA HOHONSHELT

My daughter, Michelle, perhaps because she is an only child, has always had a creative mind. I laughed at her live frog shows when she was six, and on another occasion, I dutifully ate her pink, blue, and green pancakes. But my thirty-second birthday is one of my most cherished memories.

My birthday that year was not celebrated with friends and family as in years past. Michelle and I had a quiet dinner at home. She hadn't had a chance to go shopping for a gift and was disappointed that she had nothing to give me.

About seven-thirty that evening, Michelle ordered me to go to my bedroom and close the door with instructions for me to stay there until she came for me. I could hear her busily working, but I had no idea what she was up to.

Twenty minutes later, she opened my door and stood in the hallway with a dishtowel draped over her left forearm. On the floor was a "red carpet" Michelle had pieced together from various shades of red fabric scraps my sister had given her to make doll clothes. "This way, madam," she said in a very formal tone, leading the way. My carpet of honor led to a beanbag chair that she had placed in front of the television.

Beside the beanbag chair was a TV tray with a bowl of one of my favorite snacks—popcorn—a dish of melted butter, and a saltshaker. After seating me, she filled a small bowl with popcorn.

"Would you like butter and salt on your popcorn tonight, madam?"

"Why, yes, that would be very nice, thank you."

She poured the butter on the popcorn with all the finesse of a waiter in a fine restaurant. Before handing me the popcorn, she pulled the towel from her arm and spread it over my lap, as she had experienced in some of the finer restaurants we had visited. Then she filled a bowl for herself and snuggled in beside me.

We sat there together enjoying one of our favorite weekly television programs, *The Waltons*, eating our popcorn one kernel at a time with our little fingers raised, as any proper person would.

"Is your popcorn okay, madam?"

"It's the *best* popcorn I've ever eaten," I replied. *And the best birthday I've ever had*, I thought, smiling down at my precious "gift" sitting beside me.

What feeling is so nice as a child's hand in yours?
So small, so soft and warm
like a kitten huddling in the shelter of your clasp.

MARJORIE HOLMES

COOL BLADES

Pam Gross

It was a vaguely familiar feeling—a feeling of freedom experienced a lifetime ago. Motion. Speed. Wind. Excitement. Small but present danger. Oh yes! That same exhilaration that comes with competence. I was doing it!

I was rollerblading on the boardwalk at Seaside, Oregon, on a glorious late summer afternoon. Two miles of flat, smooth pavement, sunshine, ocean air. I couldn't help my smile; it was as ridiculously relentless as a yellow happy face. My body moved with relative ease and a modicum of grace. Push, glide, push, glide—don't lift the feet so high. Swing the hips. Oops! Too much push means too much glide. Let's get more control here. Up and down! Up and down! Miles and miles—every once in a while picking up the scent of a cigar as I once again whizzed past my husband reading Tom Clancy on a bench.

Getting tired, I informed my husband that on the next pass I wanted to stop.

"Okay," he said. "I'll be ready."

Stopping was not a skill I had mastered at that point. As I approached him, I slowed to a more manageable speed. He stood up, swung his arms wide, and enfolded me in a great hug.

"I am your stopping post," he whispered.

I thought, *Yes. What a wonderful metaphor. You are my safe stopping place.*

I sat for a while on the bench enjoying the moment. Some teenagers sauntered past, talking quietly among themselves. The last, a young man of about thirteen, looked admiringly at my skates, bent down, and murmured just so we could hear, "Cool blades." Then he picked up his pace to catch his friends. My husband and I said in unison, "Cool blades?"

And we laughed.

Then the sunset zealots began converging like football fans on Super Bowl Sunday. I hoisted myself off the bench to make the most of the fading light. Up and down, push and glide. Lost in the exquisite rhythm and the elegant air, I almost missed them. But out of the corner of my eye I glimpsed a bicycle surrey pulled up close to the boardwalk. Four women nestled there comfortably in that distinctly female way of companionable silence. I thought they were completely absorbed by the inch-by-inch disappearance of the day, but as I moved past, almost out of earshot, I heard the soft call of support: "You go, girl!" To acknowledge, I signaled a "thumbs up" and continued on.

Now, whenever I put on my skates, I hear the young voice saying, "Cool blades," and I smile. When I think of my husband as a safe stopping place, I smile. When I recall the soft call of support, I smile. I'm sure glad I didn't take seriously those people who predicted, "Rollerblade? You're nearly sixty! You'll kill yourself!"

Kill myself? I'd say I was perfectly *alive* that day on the boardwalk.

TEA SET TREASURES

NANCY JO SULLIVAN

The small living room was lined with card tables, all of them brimming with rose-patterned china, long-stemmed glasses, and mismatched teacups.

That Saturday morning, I had come to the estate sale in search of a coffee table. Though I was a young mother of three and our family budget was tight, each month I managed to set aside twenty-five dollars to buy second-hand treasures for our home.

The sale was crowded with bargain seekers. Finding a small pocket of space on one side of a buffet, my glance turned toward a gold tea set displayed on a tray. Drawing near, I curled my fingers around a harp-shaped handle that trimmed the polished pot of gold. From the corner of my eye, I noticed an elderly woman was watching me. She was smiling, her eyes twinkling, her wrinkled face radiating a motherly warmth.

"It's beautiful, isn't it?" she said.

The gray-haired woman looked like she was well into her eighties. Nonetheless, she was working at the sale, wearing an apron, and holding a small tablet.

"It is," I replied as I lifted the polished lids of the matching creamer and sugar bowl.

While people brushed me, measuring tablecloths and rummaging through trinkets, my thoughts began to drift. I began remembering an Easter morning when I was twelve years old. My family, all eleven of us, had just arrived at my grandmother Mema's house.

"You're all here!" Mema proclaimed as she greeted us at the back door of her kitchen.

Though Mema was hard of hearing and her back was hunched from various ailments, she loved having us over for Easter brunch. Today she was dressed in a purple-checked dress with lavender pumps. Her brown eyes, behind bifocals, were lit up like two bright stars.

"Hey, Mema," my three little brothers called out as they jumped up to give my grandmother high fives. The trio, all dressed in yellow shirts raced to the backyard for a game of baseball.

As Mema shooed my parents into the living room, assuring them she didn't need help in the kitchen, I watched my sisters rush into the sun porch for a game of Monopoly. Like me, they were all dressed in pink calico dresses, patent leather shoes, and brimmed hats with fluttery ribbons. Every Easter, all of us matched. It was a tradition. At twelve years old, I was tired of matching. All my preteen friends were wearing wardrobes of bell-bottom jeans and tie-dye T-shirts. I was almost a teenager and no one in my family seemed to notice that I had outgrown the "cuteness" of calico and that I was embarrassed to wear a hat, especially one with a ribbon. "I'm growing up!" I stammered to myself as Mema motioned me to the stove and handed me a basket of cinnamon rolls.

"Honey, could you put these on the dining room table?" she asked.

I was glad that Mema needed my help. Working with her always made me feel valued. I held my head high as I set the rolls on the table, right next to an Easter lily.

I loved the way Mema's dining room table looked on Easter. Every year she covered it with a cloth embroidered with flowers. Her centerpiece was always the same: a gold tea set trimmed with a matching creamer and sugar bowl. The set was an heirloom; no one in the family knew for sure how old it was. On ordinary days, Mema stored the keepsake in a hutch filled with antique teacups. But on special occasions, she polished it and filled the teapot with spicy tea that smelled like oranges.

That morning, like every Easter morning, the tea set adorned her table like a regal crown. My eyes grew wide as I studied every detail of the golden treasure. "It's so lovely," I told myself as sunlight from nearby windows made the teapot glisten.

Soon Mema drew near. "Who wants tea?" she called out as she briefly closed her eyes to smell the fragrant table lily.

Mom and Dad nodded from the living room.

"I'll get the cups," I said excitedly as I began handing Mema cups from the hutch.

I watched as Mema's old but skillful hands curled around the curvy handle of the teapot. Slowly, she tipped the spout as steamy tea began to brim each cup like a carmel-colored waterfall.

After passing tea to my parents, I rushed back to the dining room only to find that Mema had set another cup on the table.

"Would you like your first cup of tea?" she asked.

"Me...?" I replied. I was surprised she had asked. In my short twelve years of life, I'd only seen adults drink from the shimmering pot of gold. "Sure," I said. Mema smiled as she filled my cup and I breathed in the scent of steeped oranges. Then the two of us made our way to the living room, steadying our steps as we carried our cups.

That Easter morning, as I sat next to Mema on the living room couch, sipping tea and talking, I took off my hat and set it on the coffee table. Deep inside I knew that I would never wear it again. I also knew that something wonderful had just happened. Mema had acknowledged that I was growing up.

The Easter memory faded as my thoughts returned to the bustle of the estate sale.

"If it's too expensive, you can leave a bid," the gray-haired woman suggested as she reached into her apron pocket and handed me a bid card.

The price tag on the estate sale tea set read $150. I couldn't help but feel a little sad. Just a few months earlier, Mema had passed away. Though it was comforting to know that Mema's tea set was now being cared for by an aunt, I found myself wishing that I could afford this treasure that triggered such tender memories.

"I'm sorry," I told the elderly worker.

She just winked.

"Go ahead. Leave a bid," she said.

I smiled and shrugged my shoulders. "What do I have to lose?" I said as I began writing my name and address on the card, along with a bid of twenty-five dollars.

The next day, as I prepared Sunday dinner in my kitchen, I heard a car pull into our driveway.

My three young daughters ran to the door. "Mom. Someone brought a present for you," the girls called out. There, on my front steps, stood the aged woman I had met just a day earlier. She was holding the tea set and there was a pink ribbon tied around the teapot.

The woman went on to explain that her mother had died many years earlier and that a few remaining family members, most of them elderly, had decided that it was finally time to sell her things.

"I have no children," the old woman said as she placed the set in my hands. "I know you will cherish it," she added. For a moment, I was at a loss for words. "This means so much," I told her as the woman smiled at my girls.

With the front door still open, we watched her drive away. I began to realize that true family heirlooms hold a value that can never be measured by a price tag. For family keepsakes represent unique and precious memories that cannot be purchased, golden memories that adorn our hearts like crowns, glistening memories that remind us that we have been and always will be loved.

As I placed the tea set inside a glass-doored cabinet in our dining room, my three daughters huddled around me. Together they shared their ohhs and ahhs. I couldn't help but notice my ten-year-old daughter, her eyes wide with wonder.

"It's so lovely," she said.

Sunshine

ucking Ned in bed one night, I leaned down to kiss him good-night. Looking closely at my face, a delighted smile spread over his.

"It looks just like sunshine," he said.

"What looks like sunshine?" I asked.

And his fingers gently touched the lines going out from the corners of my eyes. With such an observation, how could anyone mind growing old?

RUTH BELL GRAHAM
FROM *IT'S MY TURN*

SNOW ANGEL

BARBARA BAUMGARDNER

'Twas the night after Christmas
And I was alone,
No one to talk to
And no one to phone.

*T*stepped out on the patio to get an armload of firewood. The brisk air hit my face with a delightful swirl of powdery snow. I hadn't realized how stagnant my house was until now. I breathed in deeply.

Instead of firewood, I reached for the snow shovel, pushing the several inches of new fallen snow to the edge of the cement pad.

Frosty flakes danced to and fro as they gently descended from the darkness into clear view by my porch light. The variety of crystal shapes must have numbered into the millions, yet they blended together as one when they touched the cold earth.

"Oh, Lord," I whispered, "Your world is like a wintry wonderland tonight, abundant with childhood memories of so many years ago."

The new snow sparkled and glistened, clean, untouched by human hands or feet, unspotted yet by chimney soot.

I returned inside the house only long enough to grab a pair of warm gloves, and a glance at the clock told me it was 9:20 P.M. Outside again, I paused for a moment, astonished at myself, wondering if I was really going to do what I was thinking of doing.

"Yes!" I said aloud. "No one will see me. I can work as late as I wish and without the scrutinizing watch or offers of help from any neighbors."

With enthusiastic resolve I rolled my first snowball, packing it tight, and I kept on rolling and packing, smoothing and firming. Finally, my snowball was large enough for the base of my snowman.

How wonderful it was to play in the snow again, not caring that my hair and coat were wet and matted with snow—not caring that I was a grandma with a child's heart.

"And how wonderful of You, Lord, to allow me to live in a neighborhood where I am safe and not afraid to go outside by myself at night to make a snowman." Psalm 91:11 came to my mind: "For he shall give his angels charge over thee, to keep thee in all thy ways."

For a moment I stopped, then excitedly began to roll the second tier of my snowman—only now I knew my creation would not be a snowman...but a *snow angel*. And my snow angel would have charge over my entryway until she melted away.

Next, a smaller snowball for a head—then wings. A large coat box contributed enough cardboard with which I fashioned wings and covered them with shiny, heavy-duty aluminum foil. Mounting them onto the waiting body of my snow creature, I stepped back to look.

A halo! She must have a halo. A trip back inside the house yielded a wire coat hanger and some more aluminum foil.

An old string mop provided hair, and the arms were created by simply poking sticks into the body, dressed with a pair of sleeves cut off an old, worn blouse. A pair of white gloves became the hands.

For the nose, a carrot; a red candle was held in her gloved hands, and two thirty-watt fuses salvaged from the kitchen junk drawer were transformed into a pair of intent, childlike eyes.

A red bead earring was perfect for the mouth, while my white crocheted shawl, interlaced with metallic gold threads, draped around my creation, added a finishing touch of elegance.

My snow angel looked as pleased as I felt when she was completed, and I stood back to admire this midnight masterpiece.

Aching, cold, and tired, I picked up an armload of firewood. A sweet sense of satisfaction enfolded me as I headed inside.

'Twas the night after Christmas
I'm not alone, you see—
My very own angel
Is looking after me.

RESCUED

JUNE L. VARNUM

FROM *STORIES OF GOD'S ABUNDANCE FOR A MORE JOYFUL LIFE*

nother sleepless night. You might as well get up and do something. You sure aren't going to sleep now—it's almost morning. Have a cup of coffee during devotions, work in the garden. Pull weeds, dig up and separate the bulbs and iris roots. Keep busy!

I lectured myself daily, but it didn't seem to help much. Since my husband's death a year earlier, I couldn't get motivated. In truth, I spent a lot of time running away: coffee at Wendy's or a drive to the mall. I didn't need a reason for the afternoon ice cream or coffee at another fastfood place—sometimes with a friend. I looked for almost anything to get away from the house and the constant reminders that he wasn't there anymore.

Suddenly the loud jangling of my phone shattered the quiet. *It's only 6:00 A.M.!*

"Hi, Gram. Did I wake you up?"

"No, Crystal, I'm up and having a cup of coffee. Are you all right? Is anything wrong?"

"No, Gram. I just wondered if you'd be able to cook a turkey for us tomorrow. I'm on the student council at our high school, and we're going to serve early Thanksgiving dinner to the people at the veterans home. If you can, could you pick up the turkey at the school office this morning?"

"Sure, Crystal. I can do that. I'll run over about nine o'clock."

My yes led to other early morning phone calls: "Gram, would you have time to make some cookies for the bake sale after the assembly this afternoon and bring them to the gym about two o'clock? Mom worked late last night, and I had a lot of homework and didn't have time this morning."

How did she have time for anything? She had a twenty-hour per week job, was in all honor classes, active in three sports, and several student activities. Her mom didn't get off work until 11:00 P.M.

Another 5:00 A.M. call and I heard Crystal's soft voice, "Hi, Gram. I'm sorry to call so early. Could you pick me up after school and help me buy materials for the Winter Fest candidate sashes? We need shiny white cloth. And, umm, would you be able to cut and sew them?"

I poured my morning coffee, grabbed my Bible and journal. Flopping down on my favorite rocking chair, I began to laugh—right out loud. *Well, Lord, no time for mall shopping and coffee and ice cream at Wendy's today. Crystal is so fun to be with. Thank You for the times other girls on those committees go with us and include me in their chatter.*

The following week my garage floor was covered with poster paper, glitter, ribbons, spray paint, yardsticks, scissors, and jean-clad teenage girls. Their music echoed off the walls; their comments and giggles bounced about like bright balloons. Occasionally, the kitchen door opened and one of the girls would call, "Gram, come see this. Do you like the color? Should we use more gold?"

How fun to be included in their Christmas tree decorating project. Their group had entered a decorating contest put on by the downtown merchants. The night of the judging, the girls invited me to join them. Bundled up against freezing winds, we wandered along the four blocks of sparkling, glittering, decorated trees. Sometimes a mittened hand reached for mine, "Are you warm enough, Gram? Are you tired?"

When the time came to leave, my granddaughter threw me a mischievous smile. "We're going to drag Main Street now."

The girls laughed as we piled into the car. *Lord, please don't let this be a mistake.* Crystal drove slowly through town as we again admired the trees. Then she turned to make the return trip. "Gram, did you and Grandpa ever drag the streets?"

"No, honey, this is my first experience."

A burst of laughter rolled from the backseat as we sedately dragged Main Street. Two hours later, snuggled in my warmest robe, ensconced in my rocking chair, I sipped a mug of hot chocolate. All at once tears welled up and spilled over. I thought about the night's experiences—and knew peace and contentment. Swallowing the last dregs of hot chocolate, I whispered, "Thank You, Lord, for Your abundance of comfort."

Each moment has its own beauty...
a picture which was never seen before,
and which shall never be seen again.

RALPH WALDO EMERSON

THE RING

YITTA HALBERSTAM AND JUDITH LEVENTHAL
FROM *SMALL MIRACLES*

As a young bride in the summer of 1972, Faith Peterson came to the Adirondack cottage of her in-laws for a visit. Her doting husband, Kevin, took her rowing in an idyllic lake framed by pastoral woods. In the boat, sighing contentedly, Faith languidly swished her fingers through the cool water, enjoying the bracing feel of the wet cold against her warm hand.

Curling up in a corner of the boat and half-dozing, Faith continued running her hand through the water until she suddenly became aware that her diamond engagement ring had slipped off her finger. "Oh no!" she shrieked to her husband as she sat bolt upright in the boat. "My ring's gone! It must have fallen into the water!"

"That's impossible," Kevin said with skepticism. "You probably left it in a drawer at the cottage."

"No," she insisted, "I never take it off, never. And besides…just as we were about to climb into the boat, a woman at the dock complimented me on it. So I know I had it on."

"But how could it have fallen off your finger, Faith?"

"My hand was in the water, Kevin, and the ring was a little loose to begin with. It must have just slipped off…"

"Okay, don't worry. I'll find it," Kevin reassured her, and dove into the shallow lake to begin searching the bottom.

All day long, he dove again and again into the crystalline waters of the placid lake, confident he would successfully ferret out the missing ring. After all, there was no powerful current coursing through the lake that could have carried the ring away, and there was little debris below the surface that could have trapped it. But each time that his head bobbed to the surface, the story was the same. "Not yet!" he would yell bravely to Faith as she sat forlornly in the boat, peering anxiously at him. "I'll find it this time for sure!" he would smile valiantly, descending into the water for yet another foray.

Finally, at nightfall, Kevin called it quits. "I'm so sorry, honey," he said to his disconsolate spouse, putting an arm around her shoulder. "I tried my best."

"I know you did, Kevin."

"And it's not as if the ring isn't insured. We'll get you another one."

"Kevin, you're sweet and I know you mean well, but another ring just won't be the same. This is the diamond you gave me when you proposed, when we pledged our eternal love. I treasured it as a symbol for its meaning and sentimental value. Any other diamond will just be an expensive rock. No, it's the original ring I want," Faith said stubbornly. "If I can't have the one I lost, then I don't want another. Let's use the insurance money for something practical, like furniture."

"Okay, honey," Kevin shrugged, too drained from the day's rigors to argue. So Faith never got a substitute—not even when they were wealthy and could easily afford one.

In 1992, when Faith and Kevin were a middle-aged couple with teenage children of their own, they took their family to the same Adirondack cottage where they had vacationed as newlyweds. Kevin had inherited it from his parents when they had died, but had since that first visit never returned to the cottage, preferring to rent it out instead. For years, they had sent their children to overnight camp, but this summer the kids had rebelled. "C'mon, Dad," they argued, "we're too old for camp. Let's go to the Adirondacks for the summer and use Gramp's cottage."

When they arrived at the cottage, Kevin was excited. "Let me take you out to the lake," he said to his kids as his wife was unpacking. "You don't mind, do you, hon?"

"No, go ahead, enjoy yourselves! It's actually much easier for me to finish when you're all out of the way," Faith said, laughing.

"Hey, Dad, can I take my fishing rod along?" asked the youngest.

"Sure, I hear the fish are really biting today."

When they returned home a few hours later, Kevin and the kids proudly held aloft their prize catch of the day: a huge trout that weighed in at seven pounds.

"Guess what's for dinner?" Kevin winked at Faith, as she directed the requisite "oohs" and "aahs" at her youngest, who was glowing with unmasked pride. "I never caught such a big one before," he said.

"It sure is a great catch," Faith agreed, as she placed the trout on a cutting board and slit it open with a knife.

"It sure *is* a great catch," she repeated, staring in shock at the entrails of the fish. With a sweeping motion of her hand, she beckoned her husband to her side.

Inside the belly of the trout was Faith's diamond ring.

EVERYTHING IN GOD'S GOOD TIME

CYNTHIA M. HAMOND

A few Christmases ago, I opened a gift from my son and daughter-in-law and was mystified to see a diaper nestled in holiday paper. Turning it over I read, "I love you Grandpa and Grandma. See you in July." Talk about fireworks! I instantly became a first time grandmother-in-waiting with all my time references shifting around that due date.

I told everyone I knew, and those who were grandparents all gave me the same glowing response. I would will my eyes not to glaze over while I listened to these sage words over and over again: "Just wait. You can't imagine the joy and love of being a grandparent."

Of course I could imagine! I had five children of my own, four nieces and seven nephews. I'd been there. I knew what it was all about. In fact, I already loved this baby!

June took more than its fair share of summer and then July trudged into August, forgetting to leave us a grandchild along its way. "Everything in God's good time," I had always taught my children, but now I was really beginning to wonder if God might just need a calendar.

Every time the phone rang I jumped up thinking, "This is it!" If I was away from home I checked for messages every half hour. Cheryl, the mother-to-be, was kind and patient with me. I did try to limit my "How are you doing?" calls to no more than four or five or six times a day. I took her to lunch, matinees, craft sales, garage sales, anything to move the days along and hoping, just maybe, I would be with her when it happened.

If you noticed all creation sang in harmony August 4, 1998, it's because that was the day Joshua was gifted to this world. He was wonderful beyond words, and I was captivated by his every sound and motion, his very scent. And the first day of his life didn't pass before I heard myself say to a grandmother-in-waiting, "Just wait. You can't imagine it." I'm not sure, but I think I saw her eyes glaze over.

When Joshua was three months old, that little family moved two hours away. We saw him as much as possible, but it was never enough. We'd call each other Papa and Grandma just to hear the words.

Of course, Joshua learned to say Papa long before he said Grandma. On the phone he'd squeal "Hi, Papa!" all through the conversation.

He could say coo-kee and point to my cookie jar. He said pease for please and included the sign language gesture his mother taught him. He said bite, ball, show, touchdown, cracker, outside, and the list went on and on. But, no "Grandma."

When Jason and Cheryl asked us to care for Joshua while they traveled to her brother's wedding, we couldn't say yes fast enough. I was reminded of the "We've Got Annie" musical number in the movie *Annie*. You know, tap dancing down the grand stairway, singing and twirling bed sheets in the air as we prepared his room. Okay, I admit, I do exaggerate a little…our stairway is more functional than grand.

The four days rushed by with swings, slides, choo-choos, playing trucks, and reading stories. He delighted us with kisses and reminded us to pray before each meal.

When we paraded him into church he pointed out every picture of Jesus. "Jethus love me," he'd announce with absolutely no doubt about his lovability status.

At home he'd stand eye to eye with the statue of Jesus in our living room. "Hi ya, Jethus," he would say trying to shake hands or get a high five.

But, still no "Grandma."

The last night of his stay came too soon. I was in my bedroom folding his little clothes fresh from the dryer and packing them for home. I was missing him already when a scraping sound coming down the hall broke my thoughts. I looked out to see Joshua struggling to pull the statue of Jesus behind him. When he saw me, he righted the statue and flung his arm around its shoulders.

He smiled up at me, "Look, Gamma. I bring you Jethus!"

My heart filled until my joy spilled over into tears. God truly uses the simple to confound the wise. Not only had Joshua called me Gamma, but he had reminded me of what being a Christian is all about.

JUST FOR TODAY

Sally Meyer

Just for this morning, I am going to smile when I see your face,
and laugh when I feel like crying.
Just for this morning, I will let you wake up softly in your flannel p.j.'s,
and hold you until you are ready to stir.
Just for this morning, I will let you choose what you want to wear,
and I will say how beautiful you are.
Just for this morning, I will step over the laundry to pick you up,
and take you to the park to play.
Just for this morning, I will leave the dishes in the sink,
and let you teach me how to put that puzzle together.
Just for this afternoon, I will unplug the telephone and keep the computer off,
and sit with you in the garden blowing bubbles.
Just for this afternoon, I will not yell once, not even a tiny grumble
when you scream and whine for the ice cream truck,
and I will buy you one, if he comes by.
Just for this afternoon, I won't worry about what you are going to be
when you grow up,
or how you might have been before your diagnosis.
Just for this afternoon, I will let you help me make cookies,
and I won't stand over you...trying to fix things.

Just for this afternoon,
I will take you to McDonald's and buy us both a Happy Meal,
so you can have two toys.
Just for this evening, I will hold you in my arms
and tell you the story of how you were born,
and how much we love you.
Just for this evening, I will let you splash in the bathtub,
and I won't get angry
when you pour water over your sister's head.
Just for this evening, I will let you stay up late,
while we sit on the porch swing and count all the stars.
Just for this evening, I will bring you glasses of water,
and snuggle beside you for hours,
and miss my favorite TV show.
Just for this evening, when I kneel down to pray,
I will simply be grateful for all that I have,
and not ask for anything,
except just one more day.

CHRISTMAS IS FOR LOVE

AUTHOR UNKNOWN

hristmas is for love. It is for joy, for giving and sharing, for laughter, for reuniting with family and friends, for tinsel and brightly decorated packages. But mostly, Christmas is for love. I had not believed this until a small elflike student with wide-eyed innocent eyes and soft rosy cheeks gave me a wondrous gift one Christmas.

Mark was an eleven-year-old orphan who lived with his aunt, a bitter middle-aged woman greatly annoyed with the burden of caring for her dead sister's son. She never failed to remind young Mark, if it hadn't been for her generosity, he would be a vagrant, homeless waif. Still, with all the scolding and chilliness at home, he was a sweet and gentle child.

I had not noticed Mark particularly until he began staying after class each day (at the risk of arousing his aunt's anger, I later found out) to help me straighten up the room. We did this quietly and comfortably, not speaking much, but enjoying the solitude of that hour of the day. When we did talk, Mark spoke mostly of his mother. Though he was quite small when she died, he remembered a kind, gentle, loving woman, who always spent much time with him.

As Christmas drew near, however, Mark failed to stay after school each day. I looked forward to his coming, and when the days passed and he continued to scamper hurriedly from the room after class, I stopped him one afternoon and asked why he no longer helped me in the room. I told him how I had missed him, and his large gray eyes lit up eagerly as he replied, "Did you really miss me?"

I explained how he had been my best helper.

"I was making you a surprise," he whispered confidentially. "It's for Christmas." With that, he became embarrassed and dashed from the room. He didn't stay after school anymore.

Finally came the last school day before Christmas. Mark crept slowly into the room late that afternoon with his hands concealing something behind his back. "I have your present," he said timidly when I looked up. "I hope you like it." He held out his hands, and there lying in his small palms was a tiny wooden box.

"It's beautiful, Mark. Is there something in it?" I asked, opening the top to look inside.

"Oh, you can't see what's in it," he replied, "and you can't touch it or taste it or feel it, but Mother always said it makes you feel good all the time, warm on cold nights, and safe when you're all alone."

I gazed into the empty box. "What is it, Mark," I asked gently, "that will make me feel so good?"

"It's love," he whispered softly, "and Mother always said it's best when you give it away." And he turned and quietly left the room.

So now I keep a small box crudely made of scraps of wood on the piano in my living room and only smile as inquiring friends raise quizzical eyebrows when I explain to them that there is love in it.

Yes, Christmas is for gaiety, mirth and song, for good and wondrous gifts. But mostly, Christmas is for love.

A DANCE LESSON IN THE KITCHEN

MARCIA LEE LAYCOCK

hat's Grandma like, Mom?"

My seven- and nine-year-old daughters lifted serious faces toward me. The question caught at my heart, but I smiled. My mother's upcoming visit was important to all of us. I hadn't seen her since before she suffered a stroke, and I was fearful. Had the effects of the debilitation changed her more than just physically? I swallowed my apprehensions and answered the question.

"You'll love her, girls. She loves you both very much."

I could see my response wasn't quite satisfactory. My daughters needed something more. I watched my oldest, Katie, do a pirouette. Her younger sister, Laura, did an attempt at a tap step. A friend had given us an old pair of shiny black tap shoes and both girls had laid claim to them, resulting in many a battle. I knew my next sentence would get their attention.

"Grandma was a dancer, you know."

The two little faces lit up, their eyes gleamed. "She was? Did she tap dance?"

"Oh yes. She won prizes for her dancing when she was young. I think I have some pictures downstairs. Let's see what we can find."

The next hour was spent peering at old black and whites. There were photos of great-grandparents and long forgotten aunts, uncles, and cousins. Fashionable thirties-style dresses and suits were modeled by my mom and dad during their dating years. There were snaps of my father in uniform at the beginning of World War II, and old photos of my siblings and myself. For me, it was a trip down the proverbial memory lane. The memories flooded back, giving a cutting edge to the fear that had been giving me chills ever since I'd heard my mother had suffered a stroke. That news felt like the slow shredding of a strong rope that had held me securely for a long time. Though she lived on the other side of the country, I still thought of Mom as a fortress to which I could run if I ever needed shelter. The thought of that fortress beginning to crumble was terrifying.

For my daughters, flipping through the old photos was an introduction to family they didn't know existed. They pointed, giggled, and continually asked, "Who's this?" Katie held one photo in her hand and peered at it. It was of three young girls, about eleven or twelve years old. My mother was the girl on the front. Her short hair was gelled into kiss-curls on her forehead and cheeks. At the bottom of the photo in fading ink were the words, "Betty Boop and Friends."

I didn't disturb Katie as she studied the pictures. When she looked up, her eyes were hopeful. "Do you think she could teach us to dance, Mom?"

I smiled. "Your grandma will need no excuse for that, Katie. She used to tap dance all the time." The memory flooded back—a slight, trim woman, holding the edges of her apron, her eyes twinkling with mischief as she did the "soft shoe" on the black-and-white tile in our kitchen.

"I'm sure Grandma will show you…"

At that moment, the realization hit again. Since the stroke, my mother's left leg and arm were paralyzed. After two years of fighting, she was now walking with a cane and a heavy brace on her leg.

"Well," I faltered. "Grandma's legs don't work like they used to, but we'll just have to see…"

The girls asked about their grandmother every day until she finally arrived. After a time of shyness that my mom quickly broke through, Katie blurted the question that had stayed on her heart. "Grandma, will you show us how to tap dance? We have these shoes..."

My mom beamed. "Oh, what wonderful taps, Kate!" She struggled out of her chair and hobbled into the kitchen. With all of us holding our breath, my mother planted her cane firmly and gave my daughters their first tap lesson.

"Step, touch, click, step, touch, click. Oh, this brace is so clumsy! But it's a very easy step, girls. Come stand beside me and try it."

As I watched them, the taps clicking on the hard linoleum, the giggles coming from all three, a quote came to mind: "Perfect love drives out fear." I realized I was seeing that truth, alive and well, dancing before me. In spite of pain, humiliation, and fear, my mother drew on love and triumphed. In that moment I knew, though the fortress that is my mother might slowly crumble, her indomitable spirit would never die. My fear turned to joy and thankfulness for this moment, a moment that was so much more than just a dance lesson in the kitchen.

It is the sweet, simple things of life
which are the real ones after all.

LAURA INGALLS WILDER

Motherhood

ONLY ONE

*Most of all the other beautiful things in life
come by twos and threes, by dozens and hundreds.
Plenty of roses, stars, sunsets, rainbows,
brothers and sisters, aunts and cousins,
but only one mother in the whole world.*

KATE DOUGLAS WIGGIN

SNOWBALLS
AND LILACS

Lisa Marie Finley

set the big manila envelope on my mother's table, continuing our ordinary conversation, trying to draw away from the importance of this package and its contents. Through sentences of chitchat, I worked up the courage until I finally asked her to open it. She did, with a Norwegian sparkle in her blue eyes, expecting a surprise. She grew quiet as she pulled out the picture inside, and saw my own dark brown eyes staring back at her in the face of another woman. The resemblance was startling, and realization swept across her face as she turned to me with joy and wonder and whispered, "Is this your *real* mother?"

Biting my lip, a trick I had learned from her to hold back the tears, I realized this wonderful woman of substance in front of me had never seemed more precious than at this moment. A flash of all the years she had spent caring for my brothers and me flickered through my mind, as well as the life she led—a life that knew no other way than to put her children and others first on a daily basis. With the knowledge of what was truly "real," I answered her with borrowed wisdom and responded, "Yes, it's a picture of my birth mother."

My search for her had been a need for self-fulfillment, to answer all those nagging questions once wondered. My inquiry had brought feelings of guilt as well. Although my parents had always encouraged me to look, saying that they were just as curious, I didn't want either one of them to be hurt in the process or to think that I loved them any less. I secretly marveled at their encouragement, and the confidence that it represented in my steadfast love for them. But after a lifetime of unconditional love and bonding, they had well earned that security. My mother's eyes saddened as I told her that my birth mother had died; both my mother and I had often hoped for the day when we would be able to thank her personally. Now that connection would never come.

On Memorial Day, I took my two young sons to the cemetery to place flowers on my birth mother's grave. We first stopped at the gravesides of my grandparents. My mother had obviously been there, having left her homemade bouquet of snowballs and lilacs—an annual tradition of hers. Year after year, I had found comfort in those flowers, always there, loved ones always remembered. They reminded me of my mother in their simple but God-given beauty. I smiled as I thought of the daffodils she gave me each birthday—one for each year of my life. When I was younger, Mom's time-honored yellow tradition had been taken for granted. Now at the age of thirty-five, I counted each one, each flower so significant. Nothing would make me happier than to adopt a little girl and continue that tradition with her.

But now was not the time to be a daughter dabbling in daydreams, but to be a mother myself. My sons tugged on my hands, playing tug-of-war with my thoughts. We hurried off to our last stop, my birth mother's grave. Our pace slowed as we neared the general location, and we solemnly walked through row after row of beautifully decorated tombstones. I knew we were looking for a plain, simple stone, without flowers.

I had formed friendships in the last several months with my birth sisters and brother. Although they deeply loved my birth mother, I knew they were not ones to visit cemeteries. Somehow that made it even more important that I come. She definitely deserved flowers, to be remembered, and so very much more. But after half an hour of searching unsuccessfully, my sons were growing impatient, so I decided I would have to come back by myself. We were just about to leave when I spotted it.

Not her name. Not an empty stone. But the same simple bouquet o. snowballs and lilacs that I had seen earlier, the ones that most assuredly had been placed there by my mother. Mom had already been there, in the morning's early hours, to show her gratitude and the respect she felt for the importance of this woman's life, and the great gift she had given.

As I knelt and closely looked at the dates, I noticed the epitaph, which so appropriately read, "Beloved Mother." Biting my lip, I couldn't hold back the tears as I honored this remarkable woman who had given me life, and my own beloved mother, who had given that life such meaning.

Of all the friends we have,
our mother is the most loyal,
the most steadfast.
Her love knows no limit.

RHONDA S. HOGAN

IT WILL CHANGE
YOUR LIFE

DALE HANSON BOURKE
FROM *EVERYDAY MIRACLES: HOLY MOMENTS IN A MOTHER'S DAY*

*T*ime is running out for my friend. We are sitting at lunch when she casually mentions that she and her husband are thinking of "starting a family." What she means is that her biological clock has begun its countdown and she is being forced to consider the prospect of motherhood.

"We're taking a survey," she says, half-joking. "Do you think I should have a baby?"

"It will change your life," I say carefully, keeping my tone neutral.

"I know," she says. "No more sleeping in on the weekend, no more spontaneous vacations…"

But that is not what I meant at all. I look at my friend, trying to decide what to tell her.

I want her to know what she will never learn in childbirth classes. I want to tell her that the physical wounds of childbearing heal, but that becoming a mother will leave her with an emotional wound so raw that she will be forever vulnerable.

I consider warning her that she will never read a newspaper again without asking, "What if that had been my child?" That every plane crash, every fire will haunt her. That when she sees pictures of starving children, she will look at the mothers and wonder if anything could be worse than watching your child die.

I look at her carefully manicured nails and stylish suit and think that no matter how sophisticated she is, becoming a mother will reduce her to the primitive level of a she-bear protecting her cub. That a slightly urgent call of "Mom!" will cause her to drop a soufflé or her best crystal without a moment's hesitation. That the anger she will feel if that call came over a lost toy will be a joy she has never before experienced.

I feel I should warn her that no matter how many years she has invested in her career, she will be professionally derailed by motherhood. She might successfully arrange for childcare, but one day she will be waiting to go into an important business meeting, and she will think about her baby's sweet smell. She will have to use every ounce of discipline to keep from running home, just to make sure her baby is all right.

I want my friend to know that everyday routine decisions will no longer be routine. That a visit to McDonald's and a five-year-old boy's understandable desire to go to the men's room rather than the women's will become a major dilemma. That right there, in the midst of clattering trays and screaming children, issues of independence and gender identity will be weighed against the prospect that a child molester may be lurking in that restroom. I want her to know that however decisive she may be at the office, she will second-guess herself constantly as a mother.

Looking at my friend, I want to assure her that eventually she will shed the pounds of pregnancy, but she will never feel the same about herself. That her life, now so important, will be of less value to her once she has a child. That she would give it up in a moment to save her offspring, but will also begin to hope for more years, not so much to accomplish her own dreams, but to watch her child accomplish his. I want her to know that a cesarean scar or shiny stretch marks will become badges of honor.

My friend's relationship with her husband will change, I know, but not in the ways she thinks. I wish she could understand how much more you can love a man who is careful to always powder the baby or never hesitates to play "bad guys" with his son. I think she should know that she will fall in love with her husband again for reasons she would now find very unromantic.

I wish my friend could sense the bond she'll feel with women throughout history who have tried desperately to stop war and prejudice and drunk driving. I hope she will understand why I can think rationally about most issues, but become temporarily insane when I discuss the threat of nuclear war to my children's future.

I want to describe to my friend the exhilaration of seeing your son learn to hit a baseball. I want to capture for her the belly laugh of a baby who is touching the soft fur of a dog or cat for the first time. I want her to taste the joy that is so real that it actually hurts.

My friend's quizzical look makes me realize that tears have formed in my eyes. "You'll never regret it," I say finally. Then I reach across the table and squeeze my friend's hand; I offer a prayer for her and me and for all of the mere mortal women who stumble their way into this holiest of callings.

NIGHTLIGHT

SUE MONK KIDD

When I was pregnant with my daughter, my son Bob was three years old and scared of the dark. We put a nightlight in his room, but sometimes he still cried out for me in the middle of the night.

One night as I held him against me to comfort him, he touched my rounded abdomen and asked, "Mama, is it dark inside there where my little brother is?" (He was convinced that his sister was a boy.)

"Yes," I said, "it's dark in there."

"He doesn't have a nightlight, does he?"

"No, not even a nightlight," I said.

Bob patted my abdomen. I patted him. Finally he asked, "Do you think my brother is scared all by himself in there?"

"I don't think so, because he's not really alone. He's inside of me." Suddenly I had an inspiration. I said, "And it's the same way with you. When it's dark and you think you're all by yourself, you really aren't. I carry you inside me, too. Right here in my heart."

I looked into his face, wondering if he understood what I meant. He didn't say anything, he simply lay back down and went to sleep. That was the last time he called out in fear of the night.

BEDTIME BLESSINGS

NANCY JO SULLIVAN

I had a bad cold that evening, and I crawled into bed much earlier than usual. While my husband and kids watched a movie downstairs, I huddled under blankets, my body achy and chilled. A soft rain shower fell outside my bedroom window. I started to relax. The sound of the dropping rain had a soothing rhythm, a soft, pattering cadence that calmed me like a lullaby.

Just as I began drifting off to sleep, I noticed Sarah, my Down syndrome daughter standing in the doorway. With her curly hair pulled into pigtails, she was wearing a long robe and fluffy pink slippers. Her petite silhouette was shadowed by a light in the hallway.

"Mom…you…you…fforgot to tuck me in," she stuttered in a respectful whisper.

For Sarah, daily patterns and routines were very important. Even though she was sixteen years old, she still functioned at the level of a first grader. I knew this family ritual that we called "tuck-in-time" brought closure to her day and predictability to her life.

"Let's wait a while," I suggested as I motioned Sarah near. Without making a sound, Sarah sat down on the edge of my bed. For a moment, the two of us listened to the rain drumming on the roof above us.

"The rrrain is nnice," Sarah said.

I took her hand in mine. "It is," I replied as I began remembering her early childhood and the many mother-daughter moments I had spent at her bedside. Night after night, I had tucked her in, snuggling a quilt over her shoulders and tracing a small cross on her forehead.

I remembered one night when Sarah was about nine years old. I decided it was time to teach her a bedtime prayer. While Sarah nestled beneath her blankets, surrounded by pink-checked pillows and stuffed animals, I slowly repeated a rhyming passage about God and guardian angels, a simple four-line prayer.

"It's…It's…ttoo hhard ffor me," Sarah admitted with a sigh of dismay. Stroking her hair, I saw her brow wrinkle with frustration.

"Sarah, what do you want to tell God?" I asked as I gently folded her small fingers into a clasp of prayer.

Sarah closed her eyes tightly as if formulating her thoughts.

"Dear God…I…I…love…mmy mom," she said.

Throughout the years, Sarah had offered this "mom-prayer" time and time again. Though she had never learned to memorize other childhood prayers, I had grown used to this nightly routine of guiding her through simple question-answer petitions.

But now, much to my surprise, I felt Sarah tug my bedspread over my shoulders, gently and tenderly smoothing each crease of the quilt.

"Mom, what ddo you wwant to tell God?" she asked as she traced a small cross on my forehead.

I closed my eyes. I felt like an adored child. I felt safe and secure. "Dear God…I love Sarah," I said softly.

Sarah smiled. The prayer lingered. The rain continued to fall in song-like beats, covering our home and sliding down my bedroom window in small streams. So, too, a shower of love was raining down on us from heaven, blessing us.

I began to doze as Sarah quietly tiptoed to her room across the hall. I heard the squeak of her box spring and the rumpling of covers as she crawled into bed. I wondered if I should help her settle in for the night. *She's growing up…let her go*, an inner voice whispered in my heart.

Curling up in the comfort and warmth of my bed, I called out to her. "Sarah, are you an angel?" I heard her giggling. She thought I was joking.

From across the hall she called back. "I…I…am." And the rain kept falling.

MY PLASTIC PEARLS

JUDY GORDON

They brought my gift to me on Mother's Day before church. Somehow my three young sons had found six white plastic beads and had strung them together on a piece of string. Joy and pleasure shone in their big blue eyes as they proudly presented me with my "pearl necklace."

My heart was warmed and I thanked them profusely, showering them with hugs and kisses. Then I set the necklace aside as I finished getting ready for church. A thought flitted through my mind: *You should wear the necklace to church today. It would please the boys so much.* I picked it up again, taking in the scratched beads and household string. *I couldn't wear that. It looks tacky. What would people think?*

I left for church that Sunday without my pearl necklace gracing my neck. Instead of wearing my sons' handcrafted expression of love, I wore an invisible strand of fear—the fear of what people would think.

Many years later when I replay that morning and recall my concern about what people would think, I know now my response would be, "Who cares?" Today those three little boys are young men, and the string of the necklace is all tangled and twisted. It is displayed on my desk as one of my most treasured possessions and serves as a constant reminder to me: Do what is right and good, and don't worry about what others may think. Wear the plastic pearls.

Heaven's Very Special Child

A meeting was held quite far from earth,
"It's time again for another birth,"
Said the angels to the Lord above,
"This special child will need much love."
Her progress may seem very slow,
Accomplishments she may not show.
And she'll require extra care
From the folks she meets way down there.
She may not run or laugh or play.
Her thoughts may seem quite far away.
In many ways she won't adapt,
And she'll be known as handicapped.

So let's be careful where she's sent.
We want her life to be content.
Please, Lord, find the parents who
Will do a special job for You.
They will not realize right away
The leading role they're asked to play,
But with this child sent from above
Comes stronger faith and richer love.
And soon they'll know the privilege given
In caring for this gift from heaven.
Their precious charge so meek and mild
Is heaven's very special child.

EDNA MASSIMILLA

DANGER: MY MOTHER

❧

ANNE GOODRICH

Back in the midsixties my mother was still that stay-at-home mom who baked cookies, sewed, led the Girl Scouts, and volunteered for our school's Parent Teacher Association. Life was normal and suburban and good. Good that is, until the Marion Jordan PTA decided to put on a Christmas play. Oh, it's not that putting on a play wasn't a good idea to raise money for the PTA. Everyone thought performing "The Night before Christmas" would be a great fund-raiser. So did my mom—until they announced who would be playing what characters in their production.

We should have known something was wrong when my mother got home from her PTA meeting by the way the temperature dropped twenty degrees when you got within a two-foot radius of her. We finally took notice of the frosty expression on Mom's face and the firm set of her lips.

"Well, you're in the play, right?" we asked, baffled.

"Yes," was her monosyllabic reply.

"Well…what's the matter then?" one of my braver siblings inquired.

"It's who I am in the play that's the matter."

We knew she couldn't be the father, who would be reading "The Night before Christmas" to his family.

"Are you the mother?" we asked hopefully.

"No."

"The daughter?"

"No."

We were at a loss here. There was only a father, mother, son, and daughter in this production.

"Well, who are you then?"

My mother stood there, and we felt the temperature plummet another ten degrees.

"I'm the dog," was her curt reply.

"Oh." We weren't sure what to say after that. I don't think we could have said anything that would have made my mother being given the part of the family pet in the PTA play feel any better. Even Zsa Zsa, our Airedale terrier, looked sympathetic.

We three kids suddenly remembered homework that had to be done, and that Zsa's water dish needed filling, and...and whatever we could think of to quickly tiptoe out of arctic range. I mean, we could see the dilemma here. It wasn't as though we could go out bragging to all our friends, "Yep, my mom's going to be in the Christmas play this year. She's the dog." Better to just keep our noses buried in our textbooks.

However, despite feeling insulted by her part, my mother was a trooper. I think it also helped that my father, a thespian in his youth, con- vinced her that any part was worth playing well. No, my mom didn't give up and she didn't give in. She went to every rehearsal. (Just what did she practice, we wondered? Different barks?) She even told us that her dog's character had a name, Danger, which we thought was pretty apt, consider- ing. Mom even spent her own money for some kneepads after she started getting sore from running around on all fours on a wooden stage all night. And after a while, it really started to seem that my mother was enjoying this. Yes, there was definitely a gleam in her eye. We guessed that she had decided that being a canine character wasn't so humiliating after all.

It wasn't until opening night that we found out the real reason for that gleam in our mother's eye. We all went to the auditorium that evening to watch Mom perform, and it was a full house. After we settled in our seats, we opened our programs and there was Mom's name all right—"Jeanne Goodrich: Danger the Dog." We slouched down just a bit lower in our chairs as the houselights dimmed and the audience quieted. Then the big velvet curtains slowly opened with a whisper, and the play began.

It was a lovely, old-fashioned looking room, decorated for the holidays, and the Victorian-looking father announced to his family that he would read them the Christmas story. He took his seat in the big rocking chair on stage; his wife gracefully swished her long skirt and slid into the small wingback chair beside him, while the eager-looking children gathered at his feet. In the midst of this gathering around, the father called in the family dog to join them—and then came Mom. Of course, you wouldn't realize it was my mother, as she was in a brown dog costume with a big dog head and floppy long ears, and walking on all fours. But what I did recognize in the first few seconds, when Danger the dog walked out on stage, was that my mother had taken my dad's advice to heart. She was going to play her role to the hilt, with gusto. She didn't just pad onto that stage like some aging canine, but she bounced and wagged her way onto the stage to the sound of the audience's laughter.

Danger (Mom) wiggled her derriere a bit as she stretched and then settled down on the rug behind the father's chair, crossed her paws, and yawned an exaggerated puppy yawn. The laughter faded to a few subdued chuckles while the father took out a large book and began to read the familiar Christmas tale. The two children sat still, gazing in rapt attention. But not Danger. Oh no. Danger the dog was obviously too enthralled by the story to sit still.

"'Twas the night before Christmas, and all through the house, not a creature was stirring, not even a mouse…"

Danger's head suddenly lifted from her crossed paws. You could almost hear her thoughts as she turned from side to side, ears whipping around. "Mouse?! What mouse? Here? Where? I want a mouse! Where's the mouse?!"

We covered our mouths, trying to stifle our laughter.

"When up on the roof there arose such a clatter…"

Once again, Danger the dog was suddenly at attention, head jerking toward the ceiling. "What's that noise?! Intruders?! Oh boy, oh boy!" we could almost hear her say.

By this time, it was pretty obvious that most of the audience was not riveted on the recitation by the father in the play, but by the dog whose only line was a tentative "woof." And because Danger was positioned behind the other actors, they couldn't turn their heads and look at her, but it was obvious even to them that something was going on. As the reading continued, you could see how badly they wanted to make a quick backward glance as their eyeballs furtively slid over in Danger's direction.

The reading continued, and so did my mom's dog interpretation, and so did the laughter. I don't know if my mother had spent time studying our Airedale, but she had each dog nuance down pat. At just the right moment she stretched, yawned, burrowed her head in her paws, snapped her head up excitedly, and wagged her hindquarters in perfect canine imitation.

Yes, my mother was a great dog. She took what she thought was a lemon of a role, and performed it with a comedic sense that would have made Lucille Ball proud. It certainly made us proud. Almost forty years later, I still remember the time my mother was in a play, spoke not one line, and stole the show. And the Marian Jordan PTA found out that casting my mother in one of their productions was a Danger to contend with.

SCHOOL DAYS

NANCY B. GIBBS

When my twin sons started kindergarten, I followed my mother's back-to-school tradition. The entire time that we were getting ready to go and while eating breakfast, I sang the song "School Days." I don't know if I sang it to make the boys laugh, or if I was simply singing if for myself. The louder I sang the less likely I would cry. I guess you could say it was a way to cope with the fact that they were growing up.

That year sped by and the first day of the first grade was quickly upon us. Again, the morning was filled with my off-key version of "School Days."

"Oh, Mama," the boys said, while fighting back the smiles. Luckily, that simple song turned that bittersweet day into a joyous occasion for me.

Every year on the first day of school the scene was the same. Second grade, third, fourth, fifth, all the way up to the twelfth grade. I didn't care whether they liked it or not. The more they opposed, the louder I sang. Each year the song was a little easier to sing as I was learning to accept the fact that they were getting older.

Tears filled my eyes as I sang during their twelfth grade, knowing that the next year they would be off to college and I would probably not see them on the first day of college. Even though I was ready for them to grow up, I wasn't ready for them to leave home so quickly.

The night before the first day of their college classes, Chad called home. He was so excited about college and wanted to share with us all about his new books and the professors that he had met. Before we hung up, Chad said, "Classes start at 8:00 A.M. tomorrow, Mama. Are you going to call me? We have to leave at 7:30."

"Do you want me to call, son?" I asked.

"Yes, Mama, I do," Chad said. "You have to sing 'School Days.'"

"What if I just go ahead and sing it tonight, son?" I asked.

"But Mama, it just won't be the same," Chad declared.

At seven o'clock sharp the next morning I called my sons singing "School Days" to both boys on the phone. They were both laughing as we hung up. I smiled as I started my day, knowing that God had just given me a wonderful blessing. The season of my life with my boys at home was over, but an exciting new season had just begun.

One hundred years from now
it will not matter what kind of car I drove,
what kind of house I lived in,
how much money I had in my bank account,
nor what my clothes looked like.
But one hundred years from now
the world may be a little better
because I was important in the life of a child.

AUTHOR UNKNOWN

MY MOTHER PLAYED THE PIANO

JOHN SMITH AND LEANN WEISS

My mother played the piano. She played mostly by ear, I think, but she often looked at the notes, too. She played "Red River Valley," "When My Blue Moon Turns to Gold Again," and "Mexicali Rose"—but mostly she played church songs. My dad was a member of a church-songbook club of some sort, and they were always sending us a new songbook. My dad would sit in his chair for hours singing, "do-so-mi-do," as he tried to learn all the songs in the new book.

My mom played them on the piano.

As I remember, she mostly played in the early or midafternoon. During those summer months, I would approach our little white house, and through the open windows, with the white curtains moving with the breeze, I would hear her playing and singing. It was a very comforting, reassuring sound. I'm sure it brought much happiness to her.

Sometimes when I came in to get a drink or some needed thing or to ask if I could go farther than normal, she would say, "John, come here and sing this with me." She didn't say it like a command or an order or any-thing—not like when she said, "Go clean the chicken coop," or "Go hoe the garden." Those were orders. She would just say it like a request or like she would appreciate it as a favor—you know. I usually didn't want to. I was afraid my friends would hear through the open windows—or worse yet, would say, "What took you so long?" And I would sort of cringe and say, "I was singing some church songs with my mother," and they would look at me as though my driveway didn't go all the way to the street.

I made every possible excuse I could. Of course, I didn't just say *no*. You can't do that with requests, you know, and besides, I didn't say that word to my parents. The *N* word was the death word, and if I said it—even in fun—I would die.

I always knew that.

"Come on, John," she would coax, "it will only take a minute."

"Oh, Mom," I would say, "Oh, *Mother*"—the exasperation and disgust would absolutely drip from my voice, but usually I would go, dragging my reluctant feet.

She would be so enthusiastic. She would say, "Now, I want you to sing this alto part for me." And she would play it and sing it, and then she would play it while I sang it. Then she would play the soprano part and sing that—then she would play both of them and sing my part—and then she would play both parts, and I would sing alto while she sang soprano. You can't imagine how excited she would be when we finished. "Isn't that just the prettiest song you ever heard?" she would exclaim. If I thought it was something less than that—I certainly kept it to myself.

I played my role halfheartedly—at best. I had learned that the quickest way back outside was to learn my part as rapidly as possible, but sometimes I just couldn't get into it and sang so poorly and was so sour-faced and sullen that she would slowly close the book, pat me on the shoulder, and say, "You go on back to your friends now. We'll do this some other time."

Although I was a reluctant participant, the memories of playing the piano with my mother are among my sweetest. Sometimes now, when I can find a place where it is still and allow myself to be very quiet, I can see the old white house with the white curtains moving at the open windows; and through those open windows, I hear her voice and see those nimble fingers moving on the keys.

"Come on, John," she coaxes, "it will only take a minute. You sing alto—it goes like this—and I'll sing soprano. Isn't that the most beautiful song you ever heard?"

And in my mind I say, "I'm coming, Mom," and I rush to her with joy, because I know how happy it will make her. And it is, you know, the most beautiful song I ever heard.

A Breath of Time

Just yesterday I glanced outside
and watched my children play,
draped in clothes beyond their years
with dandelion bouquet.
Then as I blinked, the decades passed.
My young ones soon were grown,
more quickly than the summer weeds
among the grasses mown.
And now I watch their children dream
as only young ones can—
becoming all they wish to be,
triumphant in each plan.
Too young to know what lies ahead
these precious ones will see
that years were just a breath of time
and life—a potpourri.

CARLA MUIR

TOO MANY RIPPLES

CHERYL KIRKING
FROM *RIPPLES OF JOY*

he other day I received in the mail a "personal" letter from a well-known female celebrity. *Dear Cheryl*, it began, *Do you know what the biggest problem is for women after age thirty?*

Hmm. The biggest problem for women after age thirty…I began to wonder. Marriage and parenting concerns? Career issues? Spiritual struggles?

Nope. According to this movie-star friend, our biggest problem is gravity. Gravity! Now, I admit I'm not fond of the ravages of gravity, but I hardly consider it my biggest problem!

Nevertheless, gravity is beginning to take its toll on my fortyish body, particularly since I gave birth to my triplets. One day while I was standing half-dressed at the bathroom mirror, getting ready to go out, my then five-year-old daughter watched intently.

"Mommy," she asked, "why is the skin on your tummy all wrinkly like that?"

"Well, honey, my tummy had to stretch a lot when I was carrying you and your brothers before you were born, so the skin never quite went all the way back."

She pondered that explanation for a moment. "Kinda like a balloon that's lost its air, huh?"

What a painfully accurate description! "Uh…yes, dear, kind of like that."

"But, Mommy," she continued, pointing to my legs, "why are your knees all wrinkly?"

I looked down at my knees. By golly, they *were* getting wrinkly. Now I was starting to get a bit discouraged. This was one body part I didn't think had started to head south yet!

"Well, honey, that's just what happens to your skin when you get a little older," I replied.

She eyed me up and down for a few moments, her blue eyes widening, "Will your *whole body* get like that?"

"Yes," I sighed. "I suppose, eventually."

"Well," she said thoughtfully, "I guess your skin just gets tired and gives up, huh?"

HOW DOES SHE DO THAT?

JOHN TRENT, PH.D., WITH ERIN M. HEALY
FROM *MY MOTHER'S HANDS*

It took a little doing to reach the workbench in the garage where Mom was assembling a bouquet of Casablanca lilies. A pile of laundry pointed the way. Laundry, everywhere. And poinsettias. Two dozen, to be exact, in full Christmas bloom. And silver baskets. And floral foam. And five-gallon buckets full of red and white roses. A bolt of silver ribbon had tangled itself in a mess of floral wires and vases.

Chaos. Terrific chaos. I navigated the flower-strewn concrete toward a stool.

It was late and chilly. The scents of December and refrigerated flowers mingled with cinnamon and hot apple cider. A most wondrous smell. Mom held up five red roses next to the white bouquet. "What do you think?"

I hesitated. "Don't go overboard on the red."

"I won't. But it needs a little."

I trusted her judgment on this. I usually did, although I was getting better at trusting my own gut, too. I rested my elbows on the table and watched her work. She was right about the red. *How does she do that?* Soft Christmas music came from the windowsill. I glanced at our little portable radio. Trusty as ever.

My mind drifted. Twenty years ago, I had rested my elbows on a similar table. Mom was drawing something for her class at the university. I sat next to her in awe. The table was huge. The classroom was huge. The charcoal figures she bent over were huge. *How does she do that?*

I spent a great deal of my childhood asking that question, full of awe. Good night, Martha Stewart—you couldn't hold a candle to my mom. She knew how to make a home. My dad and siblings and I knew how to live in it. We reveled in its comfort. In her special touches. A chest of drawers bearing hand-drawn scenes from *Alice in Wonderland.* The special paper and paint in each one's bedroom. Hot candle wax shaped into something medieval before it's cooled. Household plants dangling in macramé hangers. Handel's *Messiah,* blasting us out of bed at dawn. A shadow box full of mementos from my father's Air Force career. Homemade applesauce. Decorative windows frosted with a sandblaster. Sand, tracked into the house for weeks. Sand. Everywhere, sand.

How did she do that?

Memories of home went with me to college. They stayed with me afterward. Of course they would. I weighed the aesthetics of creating a similar home against the financial cost of doing so. I was too frugal. I eschewed the extras of life. Splurging, I called it. Couldn't afford that. Not on my meager postgraduate salary. I settled for beach towels instead of curtains. Kept the bedspread I'd had since high school. Tried not to notice my blank white walls.

There is nothing wrong with simplicity (you could call it that, I suppose). But I soon missed those touches of my mother's. Touches that made a house a home. We talked about it one day when she came to visit. She had brought me a wreath for my front door. Sweet-smelling eucalyptus. I was surprised by how much I liked it.

"Give yourself permission to see that aesthetic things are important to you," she had said. The thought stopped me for a moment. *How does she do that?*

I loosened up a bit. I bought the scented candle here, the cheery flowers there. They added a lot to my own home. But not everything. I soon realized how insignificant *things* are. Their true significance lies in the memories they evoke—and create. My mother's eternal investment will never be found in material items, but in the warmth and caring they represent. Every gesture, every artistic decision, and every idea that ever took seed in her mind, all speak of her desire to create a comfortable haven for her family. Even the clutter—terrific chaos!—of the creative process testifies to her love for us.

The bouquet—white with just the right amount of red—was finished. Beautiful. She picked her way around the table and held it low at my hips. "Carry it here," she instructed. "Not too high, or you'll look nervous."

"I am nervous," I laughed.

"You're gorgeous," she said. "The most confident bride ever. Tomorrow will be a special day."

"These flowers will make it all the more special," I told her.

"Anything for you, hon." She gave me a kiss on the forehead. She'd be up for a while, putting finishing touches on other arrangements. "See you bright and early."

I made my way back through the cider scent and crawled into bed for one last night in my childhood home. Ah. Fuzzy flannel sheets. Soon I would make a home for my husband. Maybe someday children. I fell asleep thinking of creating a similar place, full of similar memories, for them. *How did she do that?*

ONLY MOM WILL DO

KIM JEPPESEN

I wasn't feeling well one afternoon, and I had decided to lie down for a while. My husband said, "No problem, honey, I'll take care of Ricky."

No sooner had my head hit the pillow than I heard my two-year-old call, "Mommy!"

My husband, with his sharpened parenting skills, took charge. "Now, Ricky," he scolded. "Mommy isn't feeling well. If you need something, Dad can get it for you. Just say, 'Dad, can you help me?'"

So, obediently, Ricky said in his best two-year-old language, "Dad, can you help me?"

Invisibly patting himself on the back, Dad leaned over to Ricky and said, "Oh yes, Ricky, what can I get for you?"

"Get Mom!"

Friendship

ENTWINED HEARTS

A friend will strengthen you with her prayers,
bless you with her love,
and encourage you with her heart.

AUTHOR UNKNOWN

CECE AND AGNES

MARY TREACY O'KEEFE

Cecelia and Agnes did not become good friends until many years after they met. Cecelia was nearly ten years older than Agnes, so they did not know each other despite living in the same rural community. Their relationship began as in-laws, brought together when Cecelia's daughter married Agnes's son. Later, after both women's husbands died, they became closer than ever, conversing several times each week and often traveling together.

In the early years of their friendship, Cecelia and Agnes saw each other mainly at family gatherings. They loved attending the various celebratory events of their children's lives. Birthdays, anniversaries, and the holidays were times of shared happiness. After the deaths of their husbands, Agnes and Cecelia consoled each other in their grief and eventually became the best of friends. They watched with pride as their children became grandparents, and every new addition to their families brought more joy. As their families became more independent, Cecelia and Agnes ventured beyond their small Midwestern hometown and explored the United States together.

After many years of enjoying each other's company, the years finally took their toll on Cecelia. As the older woman approached mideighties, her mind became more and more confused. Cecelia's family eventually had to make the difficult decision to move her to a nursing home. Agnes, on the other hand, remained busy as ever, her mind sharp and her wit quick.

A true friend, Agnes was determined to help Cecelia however she could, especially on her almost daily visits to her friend in the nursing home. For several years beyond the time when Cecelia could recognize her, Agnes kept coming to see and talk to "Cece." As Agnes approached her eighties, she wondered why Cece continued to live, it seemed, long past her prime. She commented frequently to the nurses at the home, "God must have forgotten my friend Cece. If I go first, I will tell Him to go and get her and bring her straight to heaven!" Everyone laughed, never dreaming that Agnes—a picture of health herself—would go first.

But Agnes did die first, one frigid December morning, without warning to her many friends and family members. The family was devastated at this unexpected shock. Agnes's funeral was delayed for several days. Since the weather was so cold, the ground was frozen solid.

Finally, the family was able to gather to celebrate Agnes's life. As her son and daughter-in-law prepared to leave for the church, they received a call from the nursing home informing them that their children's other grandmother, Cecelia, had just passed away.

As the news of Cecelia's death spread throughout the church during Agnes's funeral, one might have been surprised to see smiles and hear a few chuckles at such a sad event. Yet those who knew the two women well and had heard Agnes's promise to "talk to God" if she got to heaven first were immediately consoled in their grief. The two best friends were together again at last, joined with their Creator and each other forever.

VALENTINES IN A SHOE BOX

FAITH ANDREWS BEDFORD

Our grocery store is beginning to stock up penny valentines. The tiny cards always make me remember the year our teacher announced that there would be a prize for the best Valentine's Day mailbox.

Excitement mounted as we gathered around the art table. Mrs. Taylor had laid out all the basics: construction paper, foil, scissors, and glue. There were rolls of ribbon, doilies, and even some jars of glitter. All we needed was a shoe box.

Sharon Wilson asked if we could use things from home. When Mrs. Taylor said yes, competition shifted into high gear. Sharon, whose mother sewed, brought in real lace and some pink velvet. Ronnie Markham glued tiny white feathers to his box. They were from angel's wings, he said, but I knew they were from his dad's chickens. Mother bought eggs from Mr. Markham.

I noticed that Dolores Lepinski, who sat behind me, wasn't working on a mailbox. She was making valentines, but I didn't see a box anywhere.

I liked Dolores; she was smart and always knew the latest jump rope songs. But she never asked any of us over to play after school. She lived way out of town.

At recess I found her by the swings. "Have you finished your mailbox already?"

"No," she said, scuffing the ground with the toe of her shoe.

"Aren't you going to make one?" I asked, concerned about where we would put her valentines.

"I can't," she said quietly.

"Why not?" I asked, mystified. She was a wonderful artist.

"Cuz I don't have a shoe box," she replied in a heavy voice.

I was dumbstruck. Everyone had a shoe box.

"Did your mom throw them all out?" I inquired.

"No," Dolores whispered. "Mother doesn't get our shoes in stores— she buys them at yard sales and church bazaars. They don't come in boxes."

I looked down at her sneakers. They had once been white but were now gray, and one lace was knotted in the middle. I had noticed that Dolores's clothes were hand-me-downs from her sisters.

Finding Mother in the kitchen when I got home, I asked, "May I have a shoe box?"

"Didn't I already give you one?" she replied, looking confused.

"I messed it up," I said, crossing my fingers.

Mother gave me a long look then reached up to her cookbook shelf. "You can have this one," she said, taking out sheaves of recipes and handing the shoe box to me.

The next morning I bypassed the playground games of hopscotch and quickly slipped the shoe box in Dolores's desk. Later, when Mrs. Taylor announced that she was going to let us take our boxes home over the weekend to finish, there was a mad scramble for supplies from the art table.

On Valentine's Day, the students carefully placed their finished mailboxes on their desks. Mrs. Taylor walked slowly down the rows, stopping now and then to bestow a compliment. When she got to Dolores's desk, she gave little gasp. "Dolores," she said, "however did you do this?"

Dolores looked down at her lap. "Eggshells," she whispered.

"Excuse me?"

"I made it out of bits of dyed eggshells." Dolores repeated a little louder.

Mrs. Taylor held Dolores's box high. "I'm sure you all agree that this box deserves the blue ribbon."

We nodded in awe as we stared at the beautiful box. It was completely encrusted with dainty pastel hearts and flowers and made of what looked like tiny mosaic tiles.

"How'd you do that?" several voices asked at once.

"Well," Dolores began slowly, "I remembered how last year when we peeled our Easter eggs, the colored bits of shell reminded me of mosaic tiles. Remember how we studied about the Greeks using them on their floors and stuff?" We nodded. "So I soaked some eggshells in food coloring and broke them into tiny bits. Then I glued the pieces into these designs."

Mrs. Taylor applauded and we all joined in.

On our way to the bus, Dolores put her hand on my arm. "It was you, wasn't it?"

I shrugged and smiled. She gave my arm a little squeeze and slipped something into my coat pocket. On the way home, I pulled out a valentine beautifully painted in watercolors—an angel who looked exactly like me.

To this day, I always save shoe boxes. You never know when you'll need one.

Friendship is a long, sweet prayer
made up of kind acts that reach heavenward.

HEATHER HARPHAM KOPP

WHEN THE QUILT SHOW CAME HOME

JENNIFER GOTT

The morning of the quilt show, I stumbled to the kitchen to get some coffee. Mom was up already, and I poured a cup of coffee for each of us, thankful for the warmth of the cup and the awakening aroma. The early morning sun filtered in through the blinds, bright but muted, as if everything was still slowly waking from the night's slumber.

We lived in Sisters, Oregon, a small, picturesque town nestled beneath the snow-capped peaks of the Three Sisters. The community is renowned for its annual outdoor quilt show in July. The show is amazing, the entire town tucked snugly beneath lovingly stitched works of art, and thousands gather from across the nation to celebrate the art of quilt making.

My family's focus that year, however, wasn't on the upcoming quilt show. The summer had begun with the most devastating of news: My mother was diagnosed with Hodgkin's lymphoma. The cancer was aggressive, and chemotherapy began immediately. Without complaint, Mom began what would ultimately be a long and grueling schedule of treatment, culminating with a bone marrow transplant nearly a year later.

When Mom began her treatment, the doctor insisted that she had to stay away from public places. The massive doses of chemotherapy would soon ravage her immune system, leaving her with little or no resistance to illness. If the cancer didn't kill her, a cold could.

The doctor's admonition meant that Mom wasn't allowed to attend church or have visitors. She escaped the house only for doctor's visits. This separation from the world pained her even more than the side effects of the chemotherapy. She never complained, even though she is one of those people who is drawn to others. It is one of her gifts that I most admire—even when she doesn't *feel* like caring for another, she gives of herself and that person ends up feeling loved and special.

That July morning we shuffled out to the living room in slippers and robes, coffee in hand. As Mom began to raise the blind on the picture window that faced the mountains, she gasped. I walked toward her, a lump of fear rising in my throat. *What could it be?* As I followed Mom's gaze, my fear dissolved. There, draped across our lodgepole fence was quilt after colorful quilt, the corners of each swaying gently in the quiet breeze. My mom's special friend, Cathy, had quietly slipped down our drive in the cool predawn hours and hung multicolored, multipatterned quilts along the fence for Mom to discover when she awoke. The beauty of the quilts, with designs in vivid blues, yellows, and reds, was breathtaking against the natural backdrop. The rustic canvas—jagged mountain peaks, evergreens and sagebrush, the rough lodgepole fence—contrasted with the vibrant colors and patterns. Each quilt that hung delicately on our fence was an exquisite tapestry of love.

Mom, her hand over her mouth, closed her eyes, and tears escaped down her cheeks. She slowly nodded her head. The nod spoke the unsaid words: *This is just what I needed.* The love of her friend, who recognized Mom's need to feel connected to the world during her treatment, was as real as every joining stitch in those quilts. When I left for work, Mom was curled up on the couch, admiring the quilts, admiring the mountains…and, I could sense, counting her blessings.

MY FOREVER FRIEND

KRISTI POWERS

It is a friendship that almost didn't happen…but God in his infinite wisdom knew what I needed in my life—one true friend who knew everything about me, thorns and all, but still invited me to share and grow with her in this thing called life.

Len and Kathy Eisert went to the orphanage that crisp fall day with a slip of paper in their hand to see the baby boys, in the hopes of adding one to their family of three. But instead of a bouncing baby boy, the staff brought down one chubby, molasses-eyed girl. Realizing their mistake, they started to take the baby girl back to the nursery. Just before they started climbing the stairs, the dark-haired beauty chose to smile at Len with the biggest, toothless grin in the entire world. Right then and there she captured their hearts. Their immediate response was *"No, we'll take her!"* They knew that baby Rachel, as she was soon to be called, was meant for them and only them. That angelic baby was to become my kindred spirit, my forever friend.

I vividly remember the moment I first met her at the age of four. Rachel's oldest sister and my sister were getting together to play, and as my mom dropped off my sister at their house, there she was, sitting on her swing, the dark-haired beauty in contrast to my fair blond locks. From that moment on we were to be friends...bosom buddies.

One day in junior high we were riding home together from basketball practice, and Rachel's mom and she were talking about Rachel's future in basketball. Rachel had developed a noncancerous tumor on her thigh, which had been giving her quite a lot of pain. As we drove along that winter day, Rachel reached for my hand in the dark. I sat with her as she and her mom talked about the possibility of her giving up basketball. That is the way our friendship has always been, and I always hope it will be. When the dark times come, we cling to each other and hang on until the light comes again.

Rachel and I are mostly opposites. Rachel was the one who would be prepared and study hard for the PSAT tests for school. I would be beside her getting bored, circling answers just because I felt like it. Rachel was Clinton High School's class valedictorian and the first girl in our state renowned basketball program to be on the varsity team as a freshman. She was as intense as a person could possibly be. I, on the other hand, went to school to socialize and have fun and was easygoing in my demeanor and personality. I would often show up late for school throughout our senior year as I had a first hour study hall. I would meet Rachel and the principal in the hallway as I entered the school doors. I would say hi to them both and smile my most engaging smile at the principal. He would just shake his head and smile at his troublesome student. Those antics earned me the class award for Most Tardy, while Rachel received the Most Likely to Succeed award.

After graduation from high school, Rachel already had her life planned out before her; I felt confusion over my future and was scared. The day that high school started the next fall, I heard the bus as it made the usual pass by my house. From there it would rumble down the road past Rachel's house, then turn around and head back past my house again and on to school. I don't ever remember feeling so unsure of myself as I did that day. As I sprawled in my bed, the abrupt ring of the phone dragged me from my thoughts. I picked up the receiver and it was Rachel saying, "It sure feels weird not to be on that bus, doesn't it?" It was only one of many uncanny moments we have shared throughout our thirty years of friendship.

I can't remember a crucial or happy moment in my life that Rachel has not been beside me, cheering me on, holding my hand, and pointing me toward Christ. Sometimes even giving me a swift kick in the rear. Our friendship is one that even my husband does not understand. Although we are three hours away from each other, we just know when the other needs something. Somehow, God has orchestrated our friendship in a way that we will instinctively know when a phone call or card is needed to let the other know that we are there. One time we even sent the exact same card to each other *on the same day.*

When my father died four years ago, Rachel took time off work and stayed throughout the visitation and funeral the next day. Her eyes were constantly on me, and anytime I was sitting alone for an extended period of time I would find her sitting or standing next to me, holding my hand or just listening to me. My biggest tears fell when she reached me in the receiving line. "Rachel would know how I feel," I said to myself. "For she is a sister of my heart, and my dad loved her like he loved his own kids." I knew she would feel and share in my pain, and she did.

The only regret I have is that in the last few years, Rachel has been there for me much more than I have been there for her. I can't count how many times I have called her crying or hurting and she has *never, ever* given me the feeling that I was bothering her, or that she felt it was time I got over the things hurting me so deeply. I can only pray that I will be there for her—be that sounding block, confidant, and friend that she has been for me.

All these thoughts are in my head and heart as I try in my feeble way to thank Rachel for all that she has been and always will be in my life. My forever friend, if you had not been born and your birth mom had not given you up out of her love; if your mom and dad had not seen you that day and had you not captured their hearts, my life would not have been complete until I had found you. You, Rachel, are my one true friend, my forever friend. I thank you from the bottom of my heart.

TURNING THE PAGE

JAN COLEMAN

I wasn't crazy about brownies, but who can resist a plate of those warm treats from a new friend?

Jeanne first appeared right after the furniture was unloaded and welcomed me to the neighborhood. She had sunshine in her steps, and she lifted my weary heart right away.

Recently divorced, I was forced to give up my country dream home and rent a small duplex in town. On moving day, my spirits were about as high as the just cut grass in the front yard. In my former life, "single" was a name reserved for yellow slices of cheese or those classic 45 RPM records collected as a teenager. Now, to me, it was the summary of my miserable condition.

Yet, Jeanne wore singleness well. Like me, she had lost the dream of a happy marriage, but she was not flashing around her passport to pain. She was on a new journey and invited me to tag along. I signed on for a packaged tour, an all-inclusive adventure into a wonderful friendship.

Right away she got me out power walking and bike riding. "Health and happiness go hand in hand," she'd say as I huffed and puffed to catch up. We shared the same passion for old black-and-white movies, good historical novels, and marathon Scrabble games. With each year that went by,

I learned to laugh more and ponder my hurts even less.

We did everything together: took our first overseas trip, became leaders in a single's ministry at church, planned programs and outings, and wrote humorous skits to liven up the meetings, teaching us to laugh at ourselves.

My single life wasn't looking so bad after all.

Then it happened. I met Carl. I never intended to grow into a deeper friendship with him, but my years with Jeanne had opened my wounded heart to trust again. As the months went by, I knew he was the one God intended for me.

I prayed for a partner for my friend. "Please, Lord, we've been together so long, can't we transition into couplehood together, too?" Though Mr. Right never surfaced, Jeanne stayed her upbeat self and relished every detail of my courtship. Together, we planned the wedding, tried on every dress in town, and designed the invitations. Yet, we avoided any mention of splitting up the team. For the first time ever, we were at a loss for words.

The weekend before my wedding, Jeanne kidnapped me for a mountain getaway at Lake Tahoe, our last jaunt as single sisters. As we sat in front of a roaring fire, gazing at the snow-capped peaks of the Sierras, the jumbled emotions came gushing out.

"I feel like a Siamese twin," I said, "uncertain how we will change."

"Me, too," she blubbered. "I haven't wanted to think about it."

"It's so bittersweet for me." I grabbed another tissue. There would be no more 5:00 A.M. phone calls from my pal, no more pajama movie nights, or a phone message from Jeanne: "It's payback time; set up the Scrabble board. I'll be over after work."

My focus would shift to building a strong marriage; Jeanne would form a new circle of friends and activities that wouldn't include me.

This chapter in our lives was coming to a close, and it wasn't easy. Through all those years of romantic yearnings and daydreams of being married again, I never imagined it would come attached with an ache like this. How odd that the very part of my past I once scorned could now be one I cherished, all because God brought a friend into my life.

On my wedding eve, after writing my vows, I penned a letter to her. Tears flowed again as I recounted all our antics together, how she buoyed me up with her cheerfulness, how she will always have a special place in my heart that no one else will ever fill, not even Carl.

Turning the page, moving into a new chapter in my life isn't easy. Part of me yearns to draw back into the life of singleness made so comfortable with you as my sidekick. Such a cherished story written for me, but one that must come to an end because it's written by the Author of Life.

My friend, you were an example to me of trusting in the Lord, and your positive attitude was something I needed to embrace. Because of you, I learned that if I keep my face to the sunshine I won't notice the shadows. And because of you and your cooking, I learned to like brownies!

After my marriage, she gave me space to adjust to my new role. Now, we schedule time just for the two of us—a standing Scrabble date each week. Tonight, she'll bound through my front door in her sweats and get a big hug from Carl. He'll grin at us and quietly slip into the den so we can have our "friend fix." I set up the board while Jeanne slips her feet snugly into her cozy slippers and heads for the stove to brew her favorite cup of tea.

This could be a long night...and we'll enjoy every minute of it.

When Two Smiles Meet

Every friendship begins small.
Two smiles meet and
hold somehow.
But as each day passes,
amid coffee or tea,
shared secrets and phone calls,
carpools and quilting bees—
a love grows large
enough to last into eternity.

HEATHER HARPHAM KOPP

THE PIANO

SHARON SHEPPARD

I learned how to spell *yearn* in fourth grade. But I'd been doing it for a long time before I knew how to spell it. Some girls dream about having a bicycle or a horse. I dreamed about having a piano and knowing how to play it.

The closest I could come to *having* one was sitting near the front of the church every Sunday and watching Caroline Bundy's fingers fly over the keyboard. She could dress up "The Old Rugged Cross" so you could hardly recognize it. I watched her. I listened to every note. One day I said to myself, "I could do that."

On a piece of brown wrapping paper I drew myself a life-sized keyboard. I crayoned in the black keys in sets of two and three. When I had finished it, I played. As my fingers rippled up and down that paper keyboard, I could hear the songs in my head.

Sometimes on Sunday afternoons while the rest of the family napped or read Sunday school papers, I made my own instrument out of water glasses. I took eight tumblers out of the cupboard—still warm from the dishpan—and filled them with graduated amounts of water. I turned them into a scale, tapping out with a spoon all of the hymns we had sung in church that day.

When I wasn't playing my make-believe piano, I was playing with my best friend, Shirley. Shirley had a piano at her house, and every chance I got I tried it out. It wasn't as easy as Caroline had made it look. But I plunked around until I could play a tune or two.

After church one Sunday, I scooted up to Mama and whispered my secret in her ear. "I can play the piano!" I said. "Will you stay after everybody leaves and let me show you?"

"Sure, honey," she said, then went right on talking to Mrs. Harris.

Finally, when everyone else had cleared out, I led Mama up to the front pew and I slid onto the piano bench. I didn't know the names of any of the notes, but in my head I knew what the keys sounded like. I stumbled through "The Way of the Cross Leads Home," which I played on the black keys.

My mother looked a little surprised. "That's wonderful, honey!" (Parents tend to exaggerate a lot.) "How did you ever learn to do that?"

I just shrugged because I didn't know how I'd learned it.

That afternoon I overheard Mama say to Daddy, "We really need to see what we can do about getting her a piano." My heart pounded.

"That would be mighty nice, Esther, but you know we can't afford it right now," my father said.

I sighed, because I knew that was the truth. But for a minute there, I was hoping he'd say, "Yeah, sure. Let's start looking for a good used piano."

That Sunday the pastor had preached about envy. I felt guilty all afternoon because I wanted to play like Caroline. I was jealous, pure and simple. "If only I had a piano," I told myself.

Two weeks later, Shirley came over with the best and worst news I'd ever heard.

"We're moving to Northhome," she said. At first I thought she was kidding.

"Northhome?" I said. "There's nothing but ice and snow up there." (As if there was anything but ice and snow where we lived.)

"The railroad is transferring my dad."

"But you can't just leave!"

"I don't have any choice," she said. Suddenly a couple of tears trickled down her cheeks, and I knew she wasn't joking. I was about to lose my friend. I felt lost.

I didn't want to talk about it anymore. I couldn't look her in the eye. For the first time in my life, I wished she would go home. I wanted to be alone so I could cry.

"Dad says you can have our piano," she said quietly as she headed for the door. I looked at her curiously.

"What did you say?"

"My dad says you can have our piano when we move."

I think my heart stopped for a minute or so. I had to catch my breath. *"Really?"*

"Really," she said. With that she edged out our back door. I watched as she cut across the neighbor's yard, walking slowly and wiping her eyes with her mittens.

I slipped into my room and soaked my pillow with a gallon of tears. It was a little like eating sweet pickles. You're not sure whether you like them or hate them. They're a little too sour and a little too sweet to be good. While my cheeks were puckering just thinking about it, I couldn't tell which tears were sad ones and which were happy.

The day before Shirley and her family moved it was fifteen below zero. It took four men to lift and carry the piano into our living room. I was trying it out before Mama had even mopped up the melted snow they had tracked onto the linoleum.

It didn't matter that the piano was old and out of tune. It didn't matter that some of the keys stuck. It was a gift of love from a treasured friend.

Today I am a grown woman and playing piano still brings me great joy. Oftentimes, as I sit at the piano in my living room, my fingers dancing across "real" keys, I think of Shirley. Like the lovely music that always fills my home, memories of Shirley will forever fill my heart.

FRIENDSHIP FROM THE HEART

MELODY CARLSON
FROM *WOMEN ARE SISTERS AT HEART*

I remember the first time I met my husband's aunt Connie. It was my wedding day, and somehow I knew from the start this woman was special. I'd heard a little about her—how she had two grown sons, kept a beautiful home, was given to hospitality and kindness, loved to garden, and had built her own deck! I'd heard how all the kids in my husband's family loved and respected her.

Sadly, I only got to enjoy her company on rare occasions for she lived a hundred miles away, and I was soon busy raising two sons of my own, gardening, being hospitable, keeping house, and building decks.... Two parallel lives, set apart in time and space—but similar somehow, kindred—as if I were following her example without even realizing it.

Now my two sons are grown. Connie has lots of delightful grandchildren—and cancer. For over a year now, her days have been "numbered"—though God alone knows the *real* number. Yet despite her pain, she remains a striking example of a godly woman. Her faith is stronger than ever, her enthusiasm contagious, her love of life evident—only her body has slowed down a little, but not much.

Recently I took the opportunity to tell her just how much she has meant to me, to describe the quiet and profound impact she has had on my life. Of course, she just laughed, her eyes sparkling, incredulous that it could be true when we'd spent so little time together. But some things happen in a moment—in a flash. Some things you can't understand with your mind, you know them in your heart.

Treat your friends
always as if you had all the time in the world
to enjoy them.
But remember that it's the smallest moments
which often matter most.

HEATHER HARPHAM KOPP

GONE FISHIN'

CINDY WINTER-HARTLEY

*S*ince I wasn't sure we could really pull it off, I hadn't mentioned the day's plans to the boys.

I could do without the moans and groans if somehow I was unable to get all of them ready for this—a morning of fishing.

But once I announced the big event, joy filled the air. They rushed around doing their chores with rare vigor. The oldest set himself in the garage and got the gear ready. It was already near ninety degrees, but there he sat in the garage making sure we had everything. Before long we were ready to meet up with our friends.

We met them, and we all drove together. Her three sons, my three sons, my friend and I all piled into the minivan and headed to our destination. Although the boys' ages varied from two to ten years old, we all had one thing in common—we had never been fishing without the daddies. I didn't expect what was in store for us that day.

Upon arrival, we dropped our lines in the lake. Frozen corn served as our bait, and from the moment we dropped our lines in the lake, the fish grabbed ahold. Shrieks of excitement announced that we had landed another pint-sized bluefish.

My oldest son took responsibility for baiting the hooks and fixing some of the tangled lines. Without hesitation he got the fish off the hooks and released them. And when one of the younger boys caught a snapping turtle, he even held it while we took a picture. All the while leaving his own precious line behind to help the rest of us out.

But the biggest surprise happened almost without my recognizing it. I mechanically grabbed little bits of corn and baited the hook. My friend reeled out her pole and cast it out into the lake. Before we even knew it, the two of us were fishing!

The people who were having a really great time were not our sons, but rather their mothers! This morning was supposed to be for them, but something had changed. For a moment it was almost like God said that this time was for us. My morning of selfless sacrifice had been transformed.

"Behold what God has given you this day, Cindy!" I said to myself—splendid memories of me, my pal, and our kids being together.

It happens so many times that the things I do for my family somehow turn out to be equally for me. We were laughing and smiling like little nature girls. Both of us prefer eating seafood, not catching it, but on this day, we were reelin' 'em in! We prefer spas and fancy hotels but find ourselves camping several times a year. We like clean hands and peace and quiet but now get thrilled about bugs and Batman.

My friend tossed the line of her little yellow Snoopy fishing pole into the lake, tiny bits of bright yellow attached to the hook. I threw my more sophisticated line into the air and watched it unfurl and tangle the moment it landed in the water. There was no better place to be.

I will reminisce about the fish my friend caught that didn't have a lot of luck or brains and got the hook caught right near its eye. I was the one to get it out and return it to the water. I will remember the ironic moments when all the boys started throwing cheddar cheese goldfish in the water and there was a "feeding frenzy" as the real fish devoured every last one. How could I ever forget the million times I had to repair our lines? It was like getting a knot out of a really long necklace!

But what will hang on forever in my heart are the six boys, two moms, and one lake stocked full of treasures waiting for us to catch.

We went fishing for the boys and landed a marlin of memories for ourselves.

MINT FOR GOOD

RHONDA WEHLER

The long-awaited day had finally arrived. After nearly a year of separation, I would be meeting my husband of twenty years to sign away our lives together. I approached the meeting with an odd mix of dread and relief.

The months-long legal wrangling over very little of this world's goods had left me weary beyond measure. And what little self-esteem I possessed had been whittled to a thread at being discarded for someone who apparently was more gifted, beautiful, and desirable than I.

That morning I remembered the words of the Lord in the verse that had become my lifeline, "Forget the former things; do not dwell on the past. See, I am doing a new thing! Now it springs up; do you not perceive it? I am making a way in the desert and streams in the wasteland" (Isaiah 43:18–19).

Forgetting the former things wasn't yet possible for me, but I could already sense God doing something new in me and for me. But what? How could He redeem the years or make something sweet spring up from the desert that had become my life? It was more than I could comprehend, but I clung to the promise just the same.

As I prepared to leave the office for my appointment, I gazed around the room at my coworkers. Where would I be without them? As if on divine command, they had surrounded me with support and unconditional love. On days when I couldn't quite get it together, they picked up the slack. They didn't hound me for details, but were willing listeners if I needed to talk. They had even moved me into an apartment and helped me with mechanical and household problems.

With a sigh and a wave, I left the security of that room to face the difficult and final task at hand.

Closing my husband's and my joint bank accounts before an aloof professional banker seemed an anticlimactic way to end something I had devoted over half my life to. Mercifully, it was done quickly and before I knew it I was numbly driving back to the office. Although my sympathetic boss had given me the day off, I couldn't bear to face an empty apartment on this of all days.

When I walked into the office and made my way to my desk, I found there an enormous wicker basket decorated with a beautiful bow. With trembling hands I pulled off the wrapping and discovered mountains of mints (my favorite candy)—Junior mints, peppermint patties, Nordstrom mints, See's candy mints, butter mints, every kind of mint imaginable. The card tied to the ribbon read simply, "You are worth a mint to us."

Tears filled my eyes as I looked up at my smiling coworkers. It was then that I knew something sweet *would* spring up from this devastating experience. It already had.

*Happiness is a perfume you cannot pour on others
without getting a few drops on yourself.*

GEORGE BERNARD SHAW

GOOD FRIEND

YITTA HALBERSTAM MANDELBAUM
FROM *SMALL MIRACLES*

In September 1995, my eight-year-old son came home from school one day to report excitedly that a new kid from overseas had just joined his class. "This kid," he told me happily, "is just like me in every way. It's really cool, Mom," he said. "Josh loves basketball, he's great at sports, he's mischievous, he's funny, and he knows how to play great tricks on the teachers!" (Terrific! Now the poor souls would have to contend with a devilish duo instead of just one menace who had previously operated solo!) Sure enough, the two fun-loving, spirited imps teamed up for a series of hijinks, innocent pranks, and frolicking escapades that had the school staff reeling. My son was ecstatic about his new friend. "It's amazing how much he's like me," he constantly commented, in a tone of wonderment and delighted surprise.

One day, my son came home with Josh to work on a school project together. Since he lived in a different neighborhood, Josh asked if I could drive him home when they were done, and I readily agreed. When I pulled up at his address, he asked if I would like to come in and meet his mother. The hour was late, but never one to rebuff a child, I obligingly climbed out of the car. Josh ushered me into the living room and went to find his mother. "Eli's mother is here!" I heard him call to her. "Come meet her…you'll love her!"

Quick, light footsteps danced down the stairs and I turned to meet Josh's mother. She blinked. I blinked. Her jaw dropped. My mouth gaped open. Her eyes filled with tears. I tried hard to muffle a sob. Then we simultaneously ran toward each other and embraced for a long time.

Josh stood staring at this scene transfixed and perplexed. "What's going on?" he asked.

"Oh, Josh!" his mother exclaimed laughing, wiping away a tear. "Eli's mother and I were best friends in high school. After graduation, I moved abroad and I met Dad and lived overseas for years. I haven't seen Yitta for twenty-two years!"

Of course, I hadn't had an inkling. How could I have known? It was his father's surname—"Goodfriend"—that Josh used, not his mother's maiden name, although perhaps, on second thought, the name should have provided me with a slight suspicion, if not a telltale clue!

Inspiration

CHOSEN SHELTER

That little bird has chosen his shelter,
Above it are the stars and the deep heaven of worlds;
He is rocking himself to sleep without caring for tomorrow's lodging,
Calmly clinging to his little twig and leaving God to think for him.

MARTIN LUTHER

TWO SCOOPS OF ICE CREAM

CYNTHIA M. HAMOND

wo scoops please, Mr. Mason." Reggie's missing front teeth adds a lisp to his words. He counts his five pennies onto the drugstore counter. He had clutched the pennies so tightly the four blocks from home that their circle imprints and metallic scent were left on the palm of his hand.

"I know, I know." Mr. Mason punches the five-cent key, tosses the pennies into the till, and slams it closed. "It's the same every Saturday night, isn't it? One scoop strawberry with one scoop maple nut on top."

The ceiling fan overhead barely turns the humid August air. The wood floorboards squeak under Reggie's shifting feet. He knows there is no way to hurry Mr. Mason through his weekly lecture. Reggie waits respectfully, as his mother would want him to.

"You children these days. As if these times aren't hard enough!" Mr. Mason dishes out his criticism with the cone. "Your father hurt in the mine cave-in and your mama not well. This ice cream will be gone in minutes. You could have bought something useful, something to help out your mama."

"Yes, Mr. Mason," Reggie nods without really hearing. His focus is on the nearly ready to drip ice cream.

Mr. Mason finally hands the cone to him. "After all, your family works hard for what little they have, every penny of it."

"Yes, Mr. Mason," Reggie agrees before taking the cone and hurrying home.

Reggie knows that Mr. Mason is right. His family does work hard for every penny they earn. All families do. "It's hard times," the adults say to each other.

Reggie wanted to help his family. He was the youngest of nine, and it was hard to watch his older brothers and sisters all working, but seven years old is too young to go down into the mines with his brothers. So, when the posters went up all over town explaining that the gophers were ruining what scanty crop there was and offering to pay a penny a gopher tail, Reggie was excited that he had finally found a way to earn some money.

Every day, after hauling water, feeding the chickens and gathering their eggs, hoeing in the acre garden and helping his mother gather the ripened vegetables, Reggie would grab some bread and cheese and a jar of water and set off into the prairie scrub to catch gophers.

The sun was at its highest and hottest, and the prairie wind kicked up the dust from the dry ground. The grasshoppers raised out of the fields one jump ahead of his every step.

Lying in the sticker grass, Reggie would wait patiently for the gophers to come out of their holes. All day he caught gophers, and every Saturday morning he would proudly turn over his money to Mama, all except five pennies.

"Bless you, Reggie," his mother smiled down at him as the coins clanked into the baking powder tin she used for savings.

Reggie runs up the pebble walk and slams through the front screen door of home. His lungs work to suck in the thick summer air. He heads straight back to the bedroom where he can finally savor the prize of his hard work. The maple nut has dripped down onto the strawberry until there is just a hint of pink showing through, but he has made it home without losing any of the cone.

"Reggie." His mama opens her eyes and pulls herself up in bed. "Oh,

Reggie, again you bring me ice cream!"

The dripping cone leaves no time for arguing over who should eat it. His mother takes the cone and pats the bed for him to sit next to her.

Reggie climbs up and snuggles into her.

"My favorite flavors. You always remember." His mother's love floods through him.

"I'll always remember, Mama," he said.

And even these sixty years later, he always has.

If I can put one touch of a rosy sunset into the life of any man or woman, I shall feel I have worked with God.

GEORGE MACDONALD

CARL'S GARDEN

AUTHOR UNKNOWN

arl was a quiet man. He didn't talk much. He would always greet you with a big smile and a firm handshake. Even after living in our neighborhood for over fifty years, no one could really say they knew him very well.

Before his retirement, he took the bus to work each morning. The long sight of him walking down the street often worried us. He had a slight limp from a bullet wound received in World War II. Watching him, we worried that although he had survived World War II, he may not make it through our changing uptown neighborhood with its ever-increasing random violence, gangs, and drug activity.

When he saw the flyer at our local church asking for volunteers to care for the gardens behind the minister's residence, he responded in his characteristically unassuming manner. Without fanfare, he just signed up. He was well into his eighty-seventh year when the very thing we had always feared finally happened.

He was just finishing his watering for the day when three gang members approached him. Ignoring their attempt to intimidate him, he simply asked, "Would you like a drink from the hose?"

The tallest and toughest-looking of the three said, "Yeah, sure," with a malevolent little smile. As Carl offered the hose to him, the other two grabbed Carl's arm, throwing him down. As the hose snaked crazily over the ground, dousing everything in its way, Carl's assailants stole his retirement watch and his wallet, and then fled. Carl tried to get himself up, but he had been thrown down on his bad leg.

He lay there trying to gather himself as the minister came running to help him. Although the minister had witnessed the attack from his window, he couldn't get there fast enough to stop it. "Carl, are you okay? Are you hurt?" the minister kept asking as he helped Carl to his feet. Carl just passed a hand over his brow and sighed, shaking his head.

"Just some punk kids. I hope they'll wise up someday." His wet clothes clung to his slight frame as he bent to pick up the hose. He adjusted the nozzle again and started to water.

Confused and a little concerned, the minister asked, "Carl, what are you doing?"

"I've got to finish watering. It's been very dry lately," came the calm reply. Satisfying himself that Carl really was all right, the minister could only marvel. Carl was a man from a different time and place.

A few weeks later the three returned. Just as before their threat was unchallenged. Carl again offered them a drink from his hose. This time they didn't rob him. They wrenched the hose from his hand and drenched him head to foot in the icy water.

When they had finished their humiliation of him, they sauntered off down the street, throwing catcalls and curses, falling over one another laughing at the hilarity of what they had just done. Carl just watched them. Then he turned toward the warmth giving sun, picked up his hose, and went on with his watering.

The summer was quickly fading into fall. Carl was doing some tilling when he was startled by the sudden approach of someone behind him. He stumbled and fell into some evergreen branches. As he struggled to regain his footing, he turned to see the tall leader of his summer tormenters reaching down for him. He braced himself for the expected attack. "Don't worry, old man. I'm not gonna hurt you this time." The young man spoke softly, still offering the tattooed and scarred hand to Carl.

As he helped Carl get up, the man pulled a crumpled bag from his pocket and handed it to Carl. "What's this?" Carl asked.

"It's your stuff," the man explained. "It's your stuff back. Even the money in your wallet."

"I don't understand," Carl said. "Why would you help me now?"

The man shifted his feet, seeming embarrassed and ill at ease. "I learned something from you," he said. "I ran with that gang and hurt people like you. We picked on you because you were old and we knew we could do it. But every time we came and did something to you, instead of yelling and fighting back, you tried to give us a drink. You didn't hate us for hating you. You kept showing love against our hate." He stopped for a moment.

"I couldn't sleep after we stole your stuff, so here it is back." He paused for another awkward moment, not knowing what more there was to say. "That bag's my way of saying thanks for straightening me out, I guess." And with that, he walked off down the street.

Carl looked down at the sack in his hands and gingerly opened it. He took out his retirement watch and put it back on his wrist. Opening his wallet, he checked for his wedding photo. He gazed for a moment at the young bride that still smiled back at him from all those years ago.

He died one cold day after Christmas that winter. Many people attended his funeral in spite of the weather. In particular the minister noticed a tall young man that he didn't know sitting quietly in a distant corner of the church. The minister spoke of Carl's garden as a lesson in life. In a voice made thick with unshed tears, he said, "Do your best and make your garden as beautiful as you can. We will never forget Carl and his garden."

The following spring another flyer went up. It read: "Person needed to care for Carl's garden." The flyer went unnoticed by the busy parishioners until one day when a knock was heard at the minister's office door. Opening the door, the minister saw a pair of scarred and tattooed hands holding the flyer. "I believe this is my job, if you'll have me," the young man said.

The minister recognized him as the same young man who had

returned the stolen watch and wallet to Carl. He knew that Carl's kindness had turned this man's life around. As the minister handed him the keys to the garden shed, he said, "Yes, go take care of Carl's garden and honor him."

The man went to work, and over the next several years, he tended the flowers and vegetables just as Carl had done. In that time, he went to college, got married, and became a prominent member of the community. But he never forgot his promise to Carl's memory and kept the garden as beautiful as he thought Carl would have kept it.

One day he approached the new minister and told him that he couldn't care for the garden any longer. He explained with a shy and happy smile, "My wife just had a baby boy last night, and she's bringing him home on Saturday."

"Well, congratulations!" said the minister, as he was handed the garden shed keys. "That's wonderful! What's the baby's name?"

It was Carl.

WITH SONGS
OF REJOICING

JOAN WESTER ANDERSON
FROM *ANGELS WE HAVE HEARD ON HIGH*

*S*he should never have waited so long to tackle the Christmas shopping, Kimberley Little reminded herself as she shifted her bundles from one aching arm to the other. She hated shopping, hated having to brave the crowds and sift through endless piles of merchandise. But there was only so much holiday gift-buying one could do through catalogs, and, of course, the children needed their annual photo taken with Santa Claus. So here she was, imprisoned in a slow-moving "Visit Santa" line, wondering if she might spend the entire holiday season in this Albuquerque mall.

She had to admit she was never "up" at this time of year, no matter how smoothly things went. Her father had died tragically in a plane crash just a few days before Christmas when Kimberley was fourteen, and although many years had passed, she never faced December without feeling echoes of that shock, sorrow, and loneliness. As her faith matured, Kimberley had gotten involved in her church, singing in the choir and teaching her young sons to pray. She didn't doubt that her father was in heaven with Jesus, or that she would see him again. But every year, as Christmas approached, the same nagging question emerged: "This is all supposed to be so wonderful. So why isn't it?"

Kimberley shifted her packages again and looked at her three young sons. Their moods seemed no cheerier than hers. One was demanding a ride on the train farther down the mall. Another was hungry. "I hate Christmas!" muttered the eldest, his lip thrust out in frustration.

Kimberley felt guilty. "Moms have so much influence on the spirit of the family," she says. "If we're just a little bit cranky, everyone picks up on it." She didn't want to spoil this season for the children. They shouldn't carry the same vague sadness that she did.

And yet... She glanced around at the other families in line. They were all like hers, she realized: the kids irritable, tired, fighting with one another, the parents grimly determined to endure.

Why are we like this? Kimberley wondered. Where was the real Christmas, the spirit of love and peace, the joyful awareness that a Savior had come into the world? How did one cut through the confusion, the fatigue, the pressure—yes, even the sorrowful memories—to find it?

Suddenly, God nudged her. "It couldn't have been anything else," Kimberley says, "because all at once I felt a little tingle, as if something new was happening. And I realized that if I wanted to feel better about myself, I had to take the first step. I had to be brave." But how?

Sing a carol... The suggestion was already in her heart. She had recently performed a solo in church. She knew how to sing.

But this noisy shopping center was not church. "Oh no, God, not me," she told Him silently. "You remember how shy I am. People will stare."

Bring Christmas to the mall. Sing.

Kimberley sighed. It was no use. She knew that Voice. And hadn't she asked Him where Christmas was?

Softly she began to sing, "Silent night, holy night..." The couple in front of her, who had been filling out a photography order form, paused and turned around.

"All is calm, all is bright..." Kimberley reached for her youngest son and picked him up. What if they threw her out of the mall for disturbing the peace?

You're bringing the peace, the answer came. *Sing.*

The children behind her had stopped arguing. "Listen," one whispered to the other. "That lady's singing."

The tips of Kimberley's ears turned red. "Round yon virgin, mother and child..." she went on. Her sons would never speak to her again.

But...was it her imagination, or did she hear another voice? And another? Yes, the couple in front of her were singing, their order form forgotten. Now the children behind her and their parents and the family next to them. Dazed, Kimberley realized that the entire section of the Santa Claus line had joined her. Even her own offspring.

It was true! Little risks could lead to wonderful things. And she *was* feeling better, her spirit soothed, her mind quieted. Maybe Christmas—and its eternal message—was simply as close as anyone allowed it to be.

Voices faded as the song ended. "Let's do 'Angels We Have Heard on High'" Kimberly suggested to the people around her. It was her eldest's favorite carol, and her dad had always liked it, too.

It was going to be a wonderful Christmas.

Light tomorrow with today.

ELIZABETH BARRETT BROWNING

God's Promise

I see Your signature
In the sunset,
Your hand rolling back
The mighty sea.
I hear Your voice
In the stillness of the night
As You whisper,
"I'll never leave thee."

JUDY GORDON

THEN THERE WAS HOPE

EDD L. BROWN

For four weeks rain had pounded Southern California, washing out the banks of a diversion dike and returning the river to its original channel. The problem? Three years earlier housing developers had filled the original channel with new neighborhoods. And now silt, mud, rocks and raging water had destroyed many homes, leaving others inundated with filth of every description.

On my sixth day as temporary local disaster relief coordinator, frustrated and tired, I felt overwhelmed with my inability to meet the residents' needs. In only two days I had authorized thousands of dollars of vouchers for housing and other living necessities. I had even dispatched National Guard helicopters to deliver food and water to stranded families and livestock, but still the situation demanded more than I could deliver.

Noticing my deteriorating attitude, my associate dropped what she was doing and sat down across the desk from me.

"Edd," she said with empathy, "we don't need another casualty. Take a break—things won't get worse while you are gone, and besides, in your present condition, you really aren't capable of helping." She was right. Reaching for my ringing telephone, she pointed me toward the exit.

It was hot and muggy as I drove through streets filled with ruined furniture, refrigerators, pictures, toys, and dead animals. Remnants of lives and stored memories were now nothing more than heaps of junk in filthy streets. Eventually I located a team of ten people I had recruited to help "mud out" the homes.

I changed into rubber boots and walked around the job site. The concrete block wall across the rear of the property, toward the river, had been knocked over. Only the top rails of swimming pool steps were visible, and the pool was filled with rock, sand, and silt. The garage and house were window-high with debris; a six-foot wall of flood water had crashed through the doors and windows. Cabinets, furniture, clothes, beds, bedding—everything was soaked, beginning to rot and in ruins.

"What about the family?" I asked.

"We haven't seen them, but I don't know how they will react when they see this," the group's leader, Joe, replied.

I visited with the crew's men and women and stayed out of the way of working shovels, front-end loaders, and dump trucks. A ten-year-old car pulled up and parked in a cleared spot in the street. Joe walked over to me. "Edd, I think they are the owners." As I walked out to the street, I thought, *This is going to be rough. Maybe I should have stayed at the disaster relief center and concentrated on paperwork.*

A six-foot man in his middle sixties got out of the car and stared at his former home. He took several deep breaths and began to shake his head. Then with a stunned expression, he walked around the car and hesitantly opened the door for his wife, also in her sixties. She held her head in her hands and I could hear her weeping.

I stood on the walk beside the car, waiting and wondering, *What do I say? What do I do?* I took a deep breath and walked over to introduce myself. "I'm Edd Brown; I am with the disaster relief team. Would you like to see what we are doing?"

"Thank you. I'm Leon," he replied. "This is my wife, Victoria." He looked around and continued, "And this is where we lived until last week." I waited in silence as they surveyed their yard, their house, and the damage around them.

"Let me introduce you to the people who are doing the work," I said.

Our crew had salvaged what they could: some clothes, some dishes, and a few pots and pans had been cleaned and safely stacked outside. I left the couple with the workers to search for what else might be salvageable and walked into the backyard.

My gut hurt. I felt helpless. What could I possibly do to help people in situations like this?

As I waded in the muck in the backyard, I noticed an eddy had formed in the flowing water near the garage. I looked down and saw some green leaves showing through the mud. With a small shovel I began to clear away rocks and mud.

Under the silt and mud I discovered a bright red rose, vibrant in open bloom. And I suddenly felt a compulsion rise inside me. I wanted to save that rose; no, I had to save that rose.

Tenderly I dug the small rosebush out of the ground and transferred it to a gallon bucket. In the kitchen, with two quarts of bottled drinking water, I washed and cleaned the rose. Then, without thinking, I walked outside where Leon and Victoria were standing and handed the bucket to Victoria. She gasped, stammered, and began to cry. I thought she was going to faint. Feeling stupid and wondering what kind of a foolish thing I had done, I started to walk away.

"Leon, it's our rose," Victoria said. She thrust the bucket into Leon's hands and rushed to me, tears flowing down her face. Hugging me, she muttered, "Thank you, thank you, thank you." A moment later I felt another arm around me; Leon had joined his wife.

Later we learned their grandson had given them the rose for their wedding anniversary on the day they moved into their new home a year past.

"We have no insurance, hardly any savings, and neither of us can work because of medical problems," Victoria said. "I was defeated; I wanted to give up. I had just turned to Leon and asked him to take me away from this mess because I could not stand to look at it any longer." She paused, choked back some tears, and focused her eyes on me. "Then you brought me our rose, and it came to me: If God would protect such a delicate little thing, He would take care of us."

Victoria held the rose as they drove away. The crew dried their eyes, and we prayed, full of wonderment and gratitude for God's presence. The team picked up their shovels, brooms, and mops and began to clean again with a new vigor.

Renewed in mind and body, but mostly in spirit, I made my way back to the disaster center. Now I was ready to face the big job.

How rare it is to find a soul
quiet enough to hear God speak.

Francois de Salignac Fenelin

BEST PRESENT OF ALL

BONNIE COMPTON HANSON
FROM *HEART STIRRING STORIES OF LOVE*

I quickly scanned the rest of my list. This was already Friday night, and because my weekend was going to be so busy, I was trying to finish my grocery shopping as quickly as possible.

What did I still need? Oh yes, flowers—for we would be visiting my in-laws that weekend for a big dual birthday celebration. Dad was now a young ninety-three: his wife, eighty-three. So after church that Sunday we planned to drive out to their home and take them out for a nice birthday dinner.

After selecting a colorful fall arrangement, I checked my list again. Birthday cards for both of them. Pushing my piled-high cart around to the greeting card aisle, I noticed a young girl there with her mother. It was hard not to. The attractive child was positively glowing with excitement as she held up two gaily colored cards. "Oh, Mom!" she bubbled. "They're both so cool. Can't I get both of them?"

Smiling, the mother shook her head. "No, darling, just one. Hurry and choose the one you want."

"Oh, but I can't choose!" Turning to me, a perfect stranger, she grinned.

"Look—aren't they both just adorable? Which one should I pick?"

I laughed. "Well, dear, that depends on who it's for. Tell me what your friend is like, and I'll give you my recommendation."

She stared at me blankly. "Friend? What friend?"

"Why, the one you're buying the card for, of course."

She giggled. "Oh, my goodness! Didn't you know? The card is for me! See, my birthday's tomorrow. So for my present this year, Mom said I could pick out any card I want all by myself. Isn't that great? Okay, Mom, I think I'll take this one." Holding tightly to one card, she put the other one back.

Hardly believing what I'd just heard, I stuttered. "W-why congratulations, dear! How old will you be?"

Hugging her mother, she said, "Eleven."

Tears sprang to my eyes. How could any child—especially an eleven-year-old—get nothing more for her birthday than a two-dollar card?

It just wasn't fair! My first impulse was to reach right into my purse, grab the ten-dollar bill tucked inside, and thrust it into this poor child's hand. After all, I'd be paying for all my own purchases by check, so I didn't really need the cash. Wouldn't that be a loving thing to do?

Then I looked at the embarrassed mother. She was probably a single mom trying desperately to make ends meet. How it would shame her if I did such a thing! So my purse stayed unopened.

"Happy birthday, dear!" I replied instead.

Mother and daughter beamed at each other. Hugging tightly to each other and to the precious card, they hurried off to the checkout stand—having already given to each other the best and most priceless birthday present in the whole world: the gift of love.

LOVE MADE VISIBLE

BOB PERKS

ho is responsible for this?" the pastor asked. "I can't believe that no one has taken care of it. I have been getting phone calls for two days. I didn't know what to tell them."

For longer than anyone can remember, the old Gospel Church atop the hill in Reddington Valley served as a beacon for those who were lost. Not just spiritually, but even as a landmark for giving directions.

"Turn down Main Street and head toward the brightest star in the sky. You can't miss it," a traveler would hear.

You see, on top of the old church steeple was a big bright star. It was all one piece and lighted by a huge light bulb. They actually had placed it up there as part of a Christmas display and never took it down.

But two days ago the bulb burned out.

The entire town was lost without it. It seemed that the locals were all turned about at night. The confusion started when someone passing through happened to stop the mayor to ask for directions.

"I looked up and pointed to the star. It wasn't there. Thinking I was facing the wrong way, I turned around looking for it but couldn't find it," he said. "I think that guy is still riding around town."

Soon the phone started ringing at the old Gospel Church. People wanted to know what happened. The problem was even the pastor didn't know. That star was just always there. He had no idea who kept it lit or where the light bulbs were. That is, until the phone rang late that afternoon.

"Pastor, I'm hoping you can help us," the man said. "This is Police Chief Robertson. We just got back from the Delaney House. We found old Jim Delaney dead. It seems he's been dead about two days."

"I'm sorry. I must tell you that I'm not familiar with the man," the pastor said.

"No one seems to be," the Chief replied. "There are no known relatives or friends available."

"Well, if it's a burial service you are looking for, I'd be pleased to do it," said the pastor.

"That would be great. But there is something else. I'd like for you to come by in about an hour if you can. The house is up the dirt road on Bishop's Hill across the valley from your church."

"I'll be there," he replied.

The pastor arrived just as Chief Robertson pulled in. "What is it you wanted me to see, Chief?"

"Come inside. I think you'll need this stuff." As they entered the home, you could see stacks of unopened mail along with various books scattered about.

"Over here, Pastor. I believe this is for you."

There on the mantle of the fireplace was a box with a small white envelope attached. It said, "From the star keeper to the Gospel Church." The note inside it read:

To Whom It May Concern:
 Back in 1950 my beautiful wife, Mildred, became ill. We could not afford to place her in a home, so for her remaining months on this earth, I took care of her. Before her illness she attended your church every Sunday. It was so very frustrating for her not to be able to go, once she got sick. But every Sunday I would position her on the front porch so that she could see the church across the valley.

It was that Christmas someone placed a star on the steeple. Every night Mildred would say her prayers while gazing out at that star. I had just pushed her chair over to the window that night. She was barely able to breathe. As I pulled the shade up I heard her quietly say, "The star. The star is gone." As I turned around, she slumped over with one last sigh. The star indeed was not lit that night.

After her burial, I approached the pastor and made a deal with him. I agreed to keep the star lit for as long as I am alive as a memorial to my wife. So many people had loved that image during the holidays that he agreed to do it.

I am near my journey's end. The church can sell my property and all I own in exchange for a favor. I have provided enough light bulbs in this box to keep the star lit for a few more years. The key to the church door is inside this envelope. Please find someone who can take on the task of keeping the star lit after my death. I loved my wife so very much. I want that star to serve as an example of what love can be.

You can say you love someone, but it's not until you show it that love is made visible.

Jim Delaney

"When did you say he died, Chief?"

"Two days ago according to the coroner."

"That's when the star burned out, Chief." The pastor looked down for a moment, then looked back up. "Consider it done, Mr. Delaney," said the pastor. "Consider it done!"

THE PERFECT DOGWOOD

CORRINA HYDE

Since the age of three, my nana had raised my brother and me. She was mother, father, mentor, and friend. Everything I ever learned about giving I learned by her example. I walked out of the hospital doors and was unaffected for the first time by the sights and smells of spring.

She was dying and had been in a coma now for days. The prognosis was not good; the family had gathered. I had stepped outside to speak my piece to God in private. Why? Not to ask why He was taking her, for He had waited patiently while I needed her. But why now…during Easter! For some, maybe the symbolism would have been comforting, but not for me.

Like most rural families in our community, we had our traditions. We gathered during the holidays like everyone else, celebrated like everyone else, and loved and fought like all those who lived around us. If anything ever set us apart, it would be the "Easter ritual." As a young child, the ritual was something that the aunts and uncles took turns grumbling about under their breath! As I became a teen with a driver's license, the ritual became for me a life lesson.

Every Easter morning before church, my nana would get up, dress, and pull her reluctant driver out the door. The search would begin for the perfect dogwood. She would climb fences, half climb trees, and jump ditches to get at a certain branch that had just the right amount of flowers on it, or was shaped a certain way. She would take the dogwood by armloads back to the waiting car, and off to the church we would go. She would then arrange the dogwood in baskets at the front by the altar.

It was beautiful and expected! I would offer to help her in her quest but was always politely turned down. I wondered if my indifference and maybe even my groaning about having to be out so early had something to do with that.

One Easter morning, as she arranged the baskets, she found that she was short some branches. She sent me back alone to get some more. At first I was just determined to get there and get back as quickly as possible so we could go home. As I started to break off branches, I thought about where they were going, who would be approving of them, and suddenly the job took on new meaning. I started to study those flowers, no wilted flower would do, no scraggly branch; I searched for the perfect dogwood.

I held my breath as I presented it to her and waited for her to either squeal with delight or to lower her head and shake it. She did neither, she just took the branches, and finished the arrangements. I felt a little let down.

That Sunday in church, I sat up a little bit straighter. I paid more attention to the people around me, waiting to hear, "Isn't the dogwood beautiful this year—just look at those branches."

It was then that I wondered if anyone even knew that it was my nana that put it there. She did it so privately, like it was only there for her enjoyment. I wondered then if anyone really cared if it was there or not. From that day forward I knew that I cared!

So I'm asking God, "Why now? Why at Easter?" With Nana gone, who would take care of the dogwood?

We buried her on Good Friday, and that Saturday I waged a war with myself. What about tomorrow, what will I do? Should I go and get the dogwood myself? No, I was not ready to fill those shoes. Should I just stay home, so as not to embarrass myself by crying uncontrollably during church?

It wasn't until Sunday morning when tradition, faith, and habit won out. I went to church, arriving a little late to avoid seeing or talking to anyone. The plan was to sneak in the back, find a seat, and fulfill my obligation.

I walked into church and literally lost my breath!

There was dogwood everywhere!

Not arranged in baskets in the front, but lining the wall, and covering the altar. It was the most beautiful tribute that has ever been paid to the most loving woman.

I never knew who did it. I thought I would never be able to tell this person or persons what their gesture meant.

Some ten years later as I returned home to teach in the school where I had grown up, I listened as the teachers, who were once my own, talked about how much I was like Nana. They all seemed to have a story to tell about how talented, kind, and generous she was. I was flattered.

I then started to tell them about the things she had done that had impacted my life, and during this, I shared the story about the dogwood lining the church from one end to the other. I talked for the first time about how I felt walking into that church and seeing it there. My voice was thick and heavy with unshed tears, and if I could have looked anyone in the eye, I'm sure they would have reflected the same.

It was at this time that I heard sobbing. I looked at the assistant librarian, who was also a fellow church member and longtime friend, and knew before she even spoke. She simply said, "We did it. My sister and I."

Unable to speak, we left the cafeteria in tears, each of us moved very deeply. I was glad that I had an opportunity to let her know how much her thoughtfulness had meant to me during one of the hardest times in my life.

Every Memorial Day I make my way home to Nana's grave where I lay a wreath of silk flowers, covered in what else—dogwood!

Somebody's Mother

The woman was old and ragged and gray
And bent with the chill of the winter's day.
The street was wet with a recent snow
And the woman's feet were aged and slow.
She stood at the crossing and waited long,
Alone, uncared for, amid the throng
Of human beings who passed her by
Nor heeded the glance of her anxious eye.
Down the street, with laughter and shout,
Glad in the freedom of "school let out,"
Came the boys like a flock of sheep,
Hailing the snow piled white and deep,
Past the woman so old and gray
Hastened the children on their way.
Nor offered a helping hand to her—
So meek, so timid, afraid to stir
Lest the carriage wheels or the horse's feet

Should crowd her down in the slippery street.
At last came one of the merry troop,
The gladdest laddie of all the group;
He paused beside her and whispered low,
"I'll help you cross, if you wish to go."
Her aged hand on his strong young arm
She placed, and so, without hurt or harm,
He guided the trembling feet along,
Proud that his own were firm and strong.
Then back again to his friends he went,
His young heart happy and well content.
"She's somebody's mother, boys, you know,
For all she's aged and poor and slow,
And I hope some fellow will lend a hand
To help my mother, you understand,
If ever she's poor and old and gray,
When her own dear boy is far away."
And "somebody's mother" bowed low her head
In her home that night, and the prayer she said
Was, "God be kind to the noble boy,
Who is somebody's son, and pride and joy!"

MARY DOW BRINE

A DAY HEMMED
IN LOVE

NANCY JO SULLIVAN
FROM *MOMENTS OF GRACE*

I pulled on a string that lit a fluorescent ceiling light and stood looking around my grandmother's basement workshop. Making my way past a worktable laden with scissors and spools, I sat down at her cast-iron sewing machine. Above the machine, a wall plaque read: A Day Hemmed in Love Rarely Unravels.

It had been a month since my grandmother Mema's death. In her last moments of life, Mema had wrapped her hand around mine. Though cancer was invading her bones, her brown eyes bore a beautiful sheen, polished from years of smiling.

"Come back for the sewing machine...it's yours," she had said.

Now, as I opened the bottom drawer of the sewing machine cabinet, I found a collection of fabric swatches, saved patches from treasures that Mema had once sewn for my family.

Although there were piles of gingham and wool and lace squares, a piece of green floral voile caught my eye. As I took the patch into my hand, I forgot that I was a wife and mother of three; now I was seventeen years old, and it was the morning of my senior prom.

Clomping down the stairs that led to Mema's sewing room, my face streaming with exaggerated teenage tears, I plopped my gown on her worktable.

"It looks awful," I wailed.

Mema put on her bifocals, carefully examining the formal I had sewn. The hem was crooked. The waistline was puckering. Threads hung from uneven seams.

Mema shook her head when she saw that I had lined the sheer green flowered bodice with bright yellow satin.

"There wasn't any green lining left; I didn't think the yellow would show through," I whimpered.

"All it needs is the loving touch," Mema said as she held a tape measure to a mismatched sleeve.

For the rest of the day, Mema and I worked side by side at her sewing machine, her shoe tapping the foot pedal as a spool of thread whirled and a needle stitched in a buzz of rhythm.

As Mema mended raveling seams, she reminisced about her past, the hard times of the Depression, losing the farm, the war.

"I sewed your mom's clothes," Mema remembered.

As I handed her pins, I nodded, but I had heard all the stories before.

Preoccupied with the present, I began to chatter on and on about my date for the prom.

"I think he likes me more than I like him," I admitted.

"Maybe the dress will scare him off," Mema joked. We laughed.

When at last the final seams of the formal were sewn, Mema held the dress up to my shoulders.

"Try it on." She looked hopeful, her brown eyes twinkling.

As I donned the refashioned gown, I danced my way past her sewing machine, my hand grazing the back of my hair like a runway fashion model. Though the yellow lining still didn't quite go with the sheer green florals, Mema's impeccable sewing had transformed my dress into a fashion statement.

"You look beautiful." Mema grinned, her aging face a sweet, unforgettable mixture of crow's-feet and smile wrinkles.

"Love you," I said as I kissed her good-bye and rushed home to get ready for the dance.

That night, my date came to the door with a huge bright pink corsage. He didn't mind that the flowers didn't match my yellow and green gown, he just kept saying how beautiful I looked.

I laughed to myself as I remembered Mema's words, "Maybe the dress will scare him off." As we drove to the prom in an expensive limousine, I got up the nerve to tell him I just wanted to be friends.

"That's okay, let's just have fun," he said.

At the dance we mingled with other teenage friends dressed in tuxedos and gowns. We laughed and danced and ate fancy hors d'oeuvres. Everyone told me how funky my dress looked.

Though it was a memorable night, I can't seem to remember what color tux my date wore or where we went to dinner or even where the prom was held. What I do remember about prom day was the special time I spent with Mema. She had given me a memory to tuck away in my heart for a lifetime, like a precious patch of fabric saved for years in a drawer. I would never forget the laughter we shared, the stories I heard, or the age-old wisdom that had rescued me from certain dress disaster. Her presence in my young life was a thread of love that would never be broken.

I slipped the prom dress patch into my pocket and lifted the sewing machine from the cabinet, carefully placing it into a case I could carry.

I took one last look around Mema's workshop. I wanted to remember the way it looked: the scissors, the spools, and the plaque on the wall.

I wanted to remember: A Day Hemmed in Love Rarely Unravels.

HEARTSONG

JENNIFER OLIVER

When I first heard my husband sing, I laughed. I thought he was kidding around. But, no, that was his real voice. Stephen couldn't quite reach the notes, and the tone of his voice, for the most part, was nasal.

I should know. I had taken voice lessons in high school through which I was able to garner the top spot in my section at a statewide singing competition. My vocal coach was skilled at extracting only the best from her students. Thus, I was a self-appointed expert in singing.

And he stunk. Not only did he sing off-key, but he sang loud. Very loud. In spite of rolling my eyes and my fingers plugging my ears, he sang as if the whole world was his audience. Sometimes he substituted words in songs just to bug me.

For thirteen years I made fun of his voice.

I, on the other hand, confined my singing mostly to the shower. I sang with the kind of full vibrato that would make Luciano Pavarotti sound like a pipsqueak. I sang better without my hearing aids because I could feel the music soar from the back of my throat into my sinus cavities where it resonated, and the shower stall provided the perfect mechanism to hear myself.

My old vocal coach had made me take an oath before I left for college that in no way should I ever stop singing. She would be sorely disappointed if she saw me now, saving my voice for a hygienic routine.

Then one day the tables turned on me. Stephen began to make fun of my singing. Whenever he walked into the bathroom and I happened to be singing at full throttle in the shower, he would yodel.

"Stop it, Stephen!" I yelled.

His yodeling drowned out my protests.

A funny thing began to happen. I started to feel a declining confidence in my singing ability. Maybe it was Stephen's yodeling. Or perhaps my hearing was getting worse. A trip to the audiologist showed that the remainder of my hearing hadn't diminished in any way. Perhaps I should have retained a vocal coach throughout my adult life.

During the planning of my parents' fiftieth anniversary, I volunteered to sing "Ave Maria," the same song that was sung at their wedding. I practiced for hours on end. The diction, the breathing patterns, all the techniques I learned had to be perfect. After all, it had been twenty years since I sang outside the shower.

My sister e-mailed me one morning, "Have you been practicing the song?"

"Yep! Every time I'm in the shower," I replied.

Her deadpan reply: "I think you should practice more than once a week. Ha ha."

One late afternoon, being pregnant with our fourth child, I was luxuriating in a deep nap. All of a sudden, a noise awakened me. Disoriented, I looked at the digital clock that informed me that it was well past eight at night.

There it was again. That noise.

It was my husband, singing the Barney song, "I Love You, You Love Me," to the boys in the bedroom next to ours. Their high-pitched voices interwove with his boisterous style of singing. It was a nightly ritual after prayers to sing the Barney song, then "Twinkle, Twinkle Little Star."

Apparently, Stephen was putting all three boys to bed for the night. I relaxed, and for the first time I listened—really listened—to the man whose singing, no matter how awful, did not matter to the boys. The enthusiasm in their untrained voices matched their father's. I lay there in the dark with tears in my eyes.

For the first time in my life I realized that music, sculpted in all forms and fashion, was born in the heart. No amount of voice training can elicit a song as perfectly as the one that wells up from the heart.

And Stephen's voice, in my expert opinion, never sounded more beautiful than that night.

I slipped out of bed to join the chorus that was my family. What may have sounded discordant to the casual observer was, in reality, perfect harmony of our hearts.

I never complained about Stephen's singing again. He yodels still. I don't mind, though. It keeps me grounded.

Many people don't realize that deaf people also sing. They feel the vibrations and use the rhythm of their hearts, and their hands illustrate the soul of music. It's mesmerizing, watching music flow through the air with style and grace.

When I sang at the gala for my parents' fiftieth anniversary, I threw out all the rules and regulations that applied to singing. I ignored the remarks I had penciled in where I was supposed to breathe, where I was supposed to hold a note and remember the correct diction. That night I just sang from my heart.

I think my old voice coach would have approved.

AUNTIE

BETTY JOHNSON

untie was my mother's sister. She never married. I first remember her coming to live with us when my brother was born. She stayed for years in a little house in the apple orchard. Mostly, she did the gardening.

As my oldest brother got ready to farm, my dad purchased a farm near us for him to run. It had old buildings on it. In order to insure the buildings, someone had to live there. Auntie volunteered. She asked if some of us six kids could come and stay with her sometimes.

Christmas was approaching when my turn came.

"What do you want for Christmas?" I asked her. I didn't know Auntie was poor. I thought she was just thrifty. My parents always gave her meat, milk, eggs, and garden things.

She just smiled as she let down her long braid from her bun. We got into our twin beds. After she blew out the kerosene lamp, I could see the moon was bright. Then I noticed Auntie didn't have a curtain on the window.

"Auntie, why don't you have curtains on your window? Do you like to see the moon smile down?"

She sleepily replied, "Some things a person can do without."

"Don't you want curtains?" I continued.

"Oh yes, I love curtains, especially those sheer ones! But they are for rich people." Then I heard a gentle snore.

I decided to get Auntie something special—but what? My thumb caught in a loose seam of Sally, my rag doll. What had my mother stuffed her with so long ago? I would look in the morning.

At first light, I heard Auntie firing up the old cookstove before going out to feed the chickens and bring in wood. Shivering, I jumped out of bed and went to the window to see what Sally was stuffed with. I pulled and pulled—it couldn't be—but it was—an old sheer curtain, yellowed with age, and torn on the bottom. What did I expect? You didn't stuff something with good material in those days. I cried because it was too old to give to Auntie for her window. Then I looked at Sally. She looked like an empty pillow case!

The door opened. Auntie was finished with chores. She came quickly to see why I was crying.

"Where did you get that curtain?" she asked excitedly. Then she saw Sally and it was quite evident.

"I thought it would work for a present for your window!"

She pulled me onto her lap and wiped my tears.

"Don't you know presents come from people's hearts? If you want me to have this for my window, I accept! It's too long, so we'll cut off the worn part. I'll stuff Sally with some cotton batting from that old mattress on the back porch. I only saved it for something to start the fire with in the mornings. By the time you get off the bus this afternoon, I'll have it all done!"

What a happy Christmas that was! True to her word, when I came into the house, she had washed and ironed that curtain and had it up! She had stuffed Sally like she promised, and Sally looked so different—yes, she had a new pinafore—pink! It was made from scraps cut from the bottom of that curtain and dyed pink with beet juice from the beets Auntie stored in the basement. It was her present to me!

"Thank you for your Christmas present!" she said softly as she smiled at the curtain. "You're just like your mother. She shares her children with me, and you shared your doll with me!"

True Love

LOVE REMAINS

In all our losses, all our gains,
In all our pleasures, all our pains;
The life of life is: Love remains.

THEODORE TILTON

AN OLD-FASHIONED LOVE STORY

SHARON SHEPPARD

*W*alter and Martha Cox lived next door in a cozy frame house where smells of hot stewed tomatoes and cherry jelly in the making spilled out onto their small back porch and into the yard. They weren't really our grandparents, but we called them Grandma and Grandpa because our grandparents were dead.

Grandma was a tiny lady, with folds of wrinkled skin and curly gray hair. She wore long print housedresses made of flour sacks, and she always had homemade donuts in a big glass jar—hard, skinny donuts dipped in sugar.

Grandpa was a milkman, tall and bald and gentle. Baggy twill pants hung from wide green suspenders on his slender frame. Each morning after Grandpa finished his chores, he came in and sat down on the kitchen stool, and Grandma lathered him up and shaved him with an old-fashioned razor.

The Coxes were devoted to each other, and I remember overhearing my father tell my mother, around the time of Grandma and Grandpa's golden wedding anniversary, that "in all those years, Walter never looked at another woman." As a child, I wasn't exactly sure what that meant, but I thought it sounded nice.

When they were in their seventies, both were stricken with cancer, and Grandpa suffered a crippling stroke. Both of them struggled valiantly, as if by sheer will they could ward off death for a while, each not wanting to leave the other alone. But one day late in the fall, when the plum and pin cherry and crabapple trees had all dropped their leaves, Grandma went home to be with the Lord.

My father went over to stay with Grandpa during the funeral. Because of the paralysis caused by the stroke, Grandpa couldn't talk, but he used an alphabet card to spell out words. As the hearse passed slowly by the house, carrying the body of the woman he had loved so deeply for fifty-plus years, Grandpa motioned for his alphabet card and spelled out the words: "Til...death...do...us...part."

Five days later, Grandpa died.

Love is like a violin.
The music may stop now and then,
but the strings remain forever.

JUNE MASTERS BACHER

BERRY MAUVE OR MUTED WINE?

T. SUZANNE ELLER

e found me weeping bitterly in the hospital room. "What's wrong?" Richard asked, knowing we both had reason to cry. In the past forty-eight hours, I had discovered the lump in my breast was cancerous; the cancer had spread to my lymph nodes, and there was a possible spot on my brain.

I was thirty-two years old and the mother of three beautiful children.

Richard pulled me tight and tried to comfort me. Many had expressed amazement at the peace that had overwhelmed me from the beginning. God was my comfort the moment before I found out I had cancer, and He remained the same after. But it seemed to Richard that all that had crashed in the few moments he had been out of the room.

He held me tight.

"It's all been too much, hasn't it, Suz?" he said.

"That's not it," I cried and held up the hand mirror I had found in the drawer. Richard was puzzled. "I didn't know it was like this," I cried.

I had found the mirror in the nightstand and was shocked at my reflection. I didn't even recognize myself. After the surgery, I groaned in my sleep and well-meaning friends had freely pushed the self-dispensing medication to ease what they thought was pain. Unfortunately, I was allergic to morphine and had swelled like a sausage. Betadine from the surgery stained my neck, shoulder, and chest, and it was too soon for a bath. A tube hung out of my side draining the fluid from the surgical site. My left shoulder and chest were wrapped tightly in gauze where I had lost a portion of my breast. My long, curly hair was matted into one big wad.

What hit me the hardest was that over one hundred people had come to see me over the past forty-eight hours, and they had all seen this brown and white, swollen, makeupless, matted-haired, gray-gowned woman that used to be me. Where had I gone?

Richard left the room. Within moments he came back, his arms laden with small bottles. He pulled pillows out of the closet and dragged a chair over to the sink. He unraveled my IV and tucked the long tube from my side in his shirt pocket. He reached down and picked me up, and he scooted the IV stand with one foot as he carried me over to the chair. As he sat me down gently on his lap, he cradled my head in his arms over the sink and began to run warm water through my hair. He poured the small bottles he had confiscated from the cart in the hall over my hair and washed and conditioned my long curls. He wrapped my hair in a towel and he carried me, the tube, and IV stand back over to the bed. All of this done so gently that not one stitch was disturbed.

My husband, who has never blow-dried his thick, dark hair in his life, took out the blow dryer and dried my hair, the whole while entertaining me as he pretended to give beauty tips. He then proceeded, with the experience of watching me for the past twelve years, to fix my hair. I laughed as he bit his lip, more serious than any beauty school student. He bathed my shoulder and neck with a warm washcloth, careful not to disturb the area around the surgery, and rubbed lotion into my skin. Then he opened my makeup bag and began to apply makeup. I will never forget the laughter we shared as he tried to apply my mascara and blush. I opened my eyes wide and held my breath as his hands shook as he brushed the mascara on my lashes. He rubbed my cheeks with tissue to blend in the blush.

With the last touch, he held up two lipsticks. "Which one? Berry mauve or muted wine?" he asked.

He applied the lipstick like an artist painting on a canvas and then held the little mirror in front of me.

I was human again. A little swollen, but I smelled clean, my hair hung softly over my shoulders, and I recognized who I was.

"What do you think?" he asked. I began to cry again, this time because I was grateful.

"No, baby. You'll mess up my makeup job," he said, and then I burst into laughter.

During that difficult time in our lives, I was given only a ten to forty percent chance of survival over five years.

That was nine years ago.

I made it through those years with laughter, with God's comfort, and with the help of a man brought into my life named Richard.

We will celebrate our twenty-first anniversary this year with our three children—our twins, who are seventeen, and our eighteen-year-old daughter.

Richard understood what others might have taken for vanity in the midst of tragedy. Everything I had ever taken for granted had been shaken in those hours—the fact that I would watch my children grow, my health, my future. With one small act of kindness, Richard gave me normalcy.

I will always see that moment as one of the kindest gestures of our marriage.

Editor's Note: This last May Suzie watched her twins, Ryan and Melissa, graduate from high school. She continues to enjoy great health. In fact, this past September Suzie celebrated her tenth year survivor anniversary and forty-second birthday on the Amazon in Brazil as part of a missions team doing medical, dental, and construction work.

Anniversary Morning

❧

Every anniversary, early in the morning, Edmund and I light a remembrance candle and recite our wedding vows to each other: love, comfort, honor, and keep… Then we open our wedding album and look at every picture from start to finish, laughing and reminiscing. Somehow, no matter what we do for the rest of the day, we both feel like newlyweds all over again.

P. KORTEPETER

BEN AND VIRGINIA

GWYN WILLIAMS

In 1904, a railroad camp of civil engineers was set up near Knoxville, Tennessee. The L & N campsite had tents for the men, a warm campfire, a good cook, and the most modern surveying equipment available. In fact, working as a young civil engineer for the railroad at the turn of the century presented only one real drawback: a severe shortage of eligible young women.

Benjamin Murrell was one such engineer. A tall, reticent man with a quiet sense of humor and a great sensitivity for people, Ben enjoyed the nomadic railroad life. His mother had died when he was only thirteen, and this early loss caused him to become a loner.

Like all the other men, Ben sometimes longed for the companionship of a young woman, but he kept his thoughts between himself and God. On one particularly memorable spring day, a marvelous piece of information was passed around the camp: The boss's sister-in-law was coming to visit! The men knew only three things about her: She was nineteen years old, she was single, and she was pretty. By midafternoon the men could talk of little else. Her parents were sending her to escape the yellow fever that was invading the Deep South and she'd be there in only three days.

Someone found a tintype of her, and the photograph was passed around with great seriousness and grunts of approval.

Ben watched the preoccupation of his friends with a smirk. He teased them for their silliness over a girl they'd never even met. "Just look at her, Ben. Take one look and then tell us you're not interested," one of the men retorted. But Ben only shook his head and walked away chuckling.

The next two days found it difficult for the men of the L & N engineering camp to concentrate. The train would be there early Saturday morning and they discussed their plan in great detail. Freshly bathed, twenty heads of hair carefully greased and slicked back, they would all be there to meet that train and give the young woman a railroad welcome she wouldn't soon forget. She'd scan the crowd, choose the most handsome of the lot, and have an instant beau. Let the best man win, they decided. And each was determined to be that man.

The men were too preoccupied to see Ben's face as he beheld the picture of Virginia Grace for the first time. They didn't notice the way he cradled the photograph in his big hands like a lost treasure, or that he gazed at it for a long, long time. They missed the expression on his face as he looked first at the features of the delicate beauty, then at the camp full of men he suddenly perceived to be his rivals. And they didn't see Ben go into his tent, pick up a backpack, and leave camp as the sun glowed red and sank beyond a distant mountain.

Early the next morning, the men of the L & N railroad camp gathered at the train station. Virginia's family, who had come to pick her up, rolled their eyes and tried unsuccessfully not to laugh. Faces were raw from unaccustomed shaves, and the combination of men's cheap colognes was almost obnoxious. Several of the men had even stopped to pick bouquets of wildflowers along the way.

At long last the whistle was heard and the eagerly awaited train pulled into the station. When the petite, vivacious little darling of the L & N camp stepped onto the platform, a collective sigh escaped her would-be suitors. She was even prettier than the tintype depicted. Then every man's heart sank in collective despair. For there, holding her arm in a proprietary manner and grinning from ear to ear, was Benjamin Murrell. And from the way she tilted her little head to smile up into his face, they knew their efforts were in vain.

"How," his friends demanded of Ben later, "did you do that?"

"Well," he said, "I knew I didn't have a chance with all you scoundrels around. I'd have to get to her first if I wanted her attention, so I walked down to the previous station and met the train. I introduced myself as a member of the welcoming committee from her new home."

"But the nearest station is seventeen miles away!" someone blurted incredulously. "You walked seventeen miles to meet her train? That would take all night!"

"That it did," he affirmed.

Benjamin Murrell courted Virginia Grace, and in due time they were married. They raised five children and buried one, a twelve-year-old son. I don't think they tried to build the eternal romance that some women's magazines claim is so important. Nor did they have a standing Friday night date. In fact, Ben was so far out in the sticks while working on one engineering job that one of their children was a full month old before he saw his new daughter. Ben didn't take Virginia to expensive restaurants, and the most romantic gift he ever brought her was an occasional jar of olives. If Virginia ever bought a fetching nightgown and chased him around the icebox, that secret remains buried with her to this day.

What I do know is that they worked together on their relationship by being faithful to one another, treating each other with consideration and respect, having a sense of humor, bringing up their children in the knowledge and love of the Lord, and loving one another through some very difficult circumstances.

I am one of Benjamin and Virginia's great-grandchildren. He died when I was a baby, unfortunately, so I have no memory of him. NaNa (Virginia) died when I was twelve and she was eighty-five. When I knew her she was a shriveled old woman who needed assistance to get around with a walker and whose back was hunched over from osteoporosis. Her aching joints were swollen with arthritis, and her eyesight was hindered by the onset of glaucoma. At times, though, those clouded eyes would sparkle and dance with the vivaciousness of the girl my great-grandfather knew. They danced especially when she told her favorite story. It was the story of how she was so pretty that once, on the basis of a tintype, an entire camp turned out to meet the train and vie for her attention. It was the story of how one man walked seventeen miles, all night long, for a chance to meet the woman of his dreams and claim her for his wife.

Love has nothing to do with
what you are expecting to get—
only with what you are
expecting to give—
which is everything.

KATHERINE HEPBURN

LOVE IN A LOCKET

GEERY HOWE

s a seminar leader, I hear a lot of stories about people's lives and experiences. One day at the end of a seminar, a woman came up to me and told me about an event that changed her life—and in the telling, touched mine.

"I used to think I was just a nurse," she began, "until one day a couple of years ago.

"It was noontime and I was feeding 'the feeders,' the elderly who cannot feed themselves. Messy work, keeping track of each one and making sure they keep the food in their mouths. I looked up as an elderly gentleman passed by the dining room doorway. He was on his way down the hall for a daily visit with his wife.

"Our eyes met over the distance, and I knew right then in my heart that I should be with them both that noon hour. My coworker covered for me, and I followed him down the corridor.

"When I entered the room, she was lying in bed, looking up at the ceiling with her arms across her chest. He was sitting in the chair at the end of the bed with his arms crossed, looking at the floor.

"I walked over to her and said, 'Susan, is there anything you want to share today? If so, I came down to listen.' She tried to speak but her lips were dry and nothing came out. I bent over closer and asked again.

"'Susan, if you cannot say it with words, can you show me with your hands?'

"She carefully lifted her hands off her chest and held them up before her eyes. They were old hands, with leathery skin and swollen knuckles, worn from years of caring, working, and living. She then grasped the collar of her nightgown and began to pull.

"I unbuttoned the top buttons. She reached in and pulled out a long gold chain connected to a small gold locket. She held it up, and tears came to her eyes.

"Her husband got up from the end of the bed and came over. Sitting beside her, he took his hands and tenderly placed them around hers. 'There is a story about this locket,' he explained, and he began to tell it to me.

"'One day many months ago, we awoke early and I told Susan I could no longer care for her by myself. I could not carry her to the bathroom, keep the house clean, plus cook all the meals. My body could no longer do this. I, too, had aged.

"'We talked long and hard that morning. She told me to go to coffee club and ask where a good place might be. I didn't return until lunchtime. We chose here from the advice of others.

"'On the first day, after all the forms, the weighing and the tests, the nurse told us that her fingers were so swollen that they would need to cut off her wedding rings.

"'After everyone left the room, we sat together and she asked me, "What do we do with a broken ring and a whole ring?" For I had chosen to take off my ring that day, too.

"'Both of these rings were old, more oval than round. Thin in some places and strong in other parts. We made a difficult decision. That was the hardest night in my entire life. It was the first time we had slept apart in forty-three years.

"'The next morning I took the two rings to the jewelers and had them melted. Half of that locket is my ring, and the other half is hers. The clasp is made from the engagement ring that I gave her when I proposed to her, down by the pond at the back of the farm on a warm summer's evening.

She told me it was about time and answered yes.

"'On the inside it says *I love you, Susan,* and on the other side it says *I love you, Joseph.* We made this locket because we were afraid that one day we might not be able to say these words to each other.'

"He picked her up and held her gently in his arms. I knew that I was the channel, and they had the message. I slipped out the door and went back to feeding the feeders with more kindness in my heart.

"After lunch and the paperwork, I walked back down to their room. He was rocking her in his arms and singing the last verse of 'Amazing Grace.' I waited while he laid her down, crossed her arms, and closed her eyes.

"He turned to me at the door and said, 'Thank you. She passed away just a little bit ago. Thank you very much.'

"I used to say I was 'just a nurse' or 'just a mom,' but I don't anymore. No one is just an anything. Each of us has gifts and talents. We need not limit ourselves by such small definitions. I know what I can do when I listen to my heart and live from there."

As she finished her story, we hugged and she left. I stood in the doorway with thankfulness.

With This Ring

"With this ring…"
your strong, familiar voice
fell like a benediction
on my heart, that dusk;
tall candles flickered gently,
our age old vows were said,
and I could hear
someone begin to sing
an old, old song,
timeworn and lovely,
timeworn and dear.
And in that dusk
were old, old friends—

and you,
an old friend, too,
(and dearer than them all).
Only my ring seemed new—
its plain gold surface
warm and bright
and strange to me
that candlelight…
unworn—unmarred.
Could it be that wedding rings
like other things,
Are lovelier when scarred?

RUTH BELL GRAHAM
FROM *RUTH BELL GRAHAM'S COLLECTED POEMS*

MOM'S LAST LAUGH

ROBIN LEE SHOPE

onsumed by my loss, I didn't notice the hardness of the pew where I sat. I was at the funeral of my dearest friend—my mother. She finally had lost her long battle with cancer. The hurt was so intense, I found it heard to breathe at times.

Always supportive, Mother clapped loudest at my school plays, held a box of tissues while listening to my first heartbreak, comforted me at my father's death, encouraged me in college, and prayed for me my entire life.

When Mother's illness was diagnosed, my sister had a new baby and my brother had recently married his childhood sweetheart, so it fell to me, the twenty-seven-year-old middle child without entanglements, to take care of her. I counted it an honor.

"What now, Lord?" I asked, sitting in church. My life stretched out before me as an empty abyss.

My brother sat stoically with his face toward the cross while clutching his wife's hand. My sister sat slumped against her husband's shoulder, his arms around her as she cradled their child. All so deeply grieving, no one noticed I sat alone.

My place had been with our mother, preparing her meals, helping her walk, taking her to the doctor, seeing to her medication, reading the Bible together. Now she was with the Lord.

My work was finished, and I was alone.

I heard a door open and slam shut at the back of the church. Quick footsteps hurried along the carpeted floor. An exasperated young man looked around briefly and then sat next to me. He folded his hands and placed them on his lap. His eyes were brimming with tears. He began to sniffle.

"I'm late," he explained, though no explanation was necessary.

After several eulogies, he leaned over and commented, "Why do they keep calling Mary by the name of 'Margaret'?"

"Because that was her name, Margaret. Never Mary. No one called her 'Mary,'" I whispered. I wondered why this person couldn't have sat on the other side of the church. He interrupted my grieving with his tears and fidgeting. Who was this stranger anyway?

"No, that isn't correct," he insisted, as several people glanced over at our whispering, "Her name is Mary, Mary Peters."

"That isn't who this is."

"Isn't this the Lutheran church?"

"No, the Lutheran church is across the street."

"Oh."

"I believe you're at the wrong funeral, sir."

The solemnness of the occasion mixed with the realization of the man's mistake bubbled up inside me and came out as laughter. I cupped my hands over my face, hoping it would be interpreted as sobs.

The creaking pew gave me away. Sharp looks from other mourners only made the situation seem more hilarious. I peeked at the bewildered, misguided man seated beside me. He was laughing, too, as he glanced around, deciding it was too late for an uneventful exit. I imagined Mother laughing.

At the final amen, we darted out a door and into the parking lot.

"I do believe we'll be the talk of the town," he smiled. He said his name was Rick and since he had missed his aunt's funeral, asked me out for a cup of coffee.

That afternoon began a lifelong journey for me with this man who attended the wrong funeral, but he was in the right place. A year after meeting, we were married at a country church where he was the assistant pastor. This time we both arrived at the same church, right on time.

In my time of sorrow, God gave me laughter. In place of loneliness, God gave me love. This past June we celebrated our twenty-second wedding anniversary.

Whenever anyone asks us how we met, Rick tells them, "Her mom and my Aunt Mary introduced us, and it's truly a match made in heaven."

Love is the master key that opens the gates of happiness.

OLIVER WENDELL HOLMES

GRACE'S AMAZING VALENTINE

❦

SHAWN ALYNE STRANNIGAN

Grace and Homer "Willy" Williamston were married on September 8, 1984. Both had lost their previous mates to cancer. In fact, Grace had provided hospice care for Willy's first wife during the final days of her life.

Almost from the beginning of their relationship, Grace and Willy had known they were soul mates. After a whirlwind courtship and joyful marriage, the couple found any and every excuse to find ways to celebrate their love.

One particular Valentine's Day, while visiting the Oregon coast, Willy breathed new life into the traditional lover's holiday.

"Willy! What's taking you so long in there?" called Grace through the bathroom door of their motel room. "I've been ready to go to breakfast for an hour."

"Hang on, Grace, I'm coming," replied Willy, sounding a bit out of breath.

Moments later, the bathroom door opened, and Grace couldn't help laughing at the sight before her. Her beloved Willy half-wrestled, half-carried a giant heart-shaped balloon through the small doorway.

"Happy Valentine's Day, Grace!" exclaimed her red-faced husband, triumphantly holding the red balloon up for his wife to admire. "I blew it up myself."

Printed across the balloon were the words, "Love You So Much It Hurts!" Underneath the words was a "Band-Aid" inside which Willy had scrawled: "To Grace, my love, from your ever-loving Willy."

After Willy caught his breath, the couple stuffed the bulky balloon into the backseat of their car, giggling like a couple of kids. Somehow, it survived the trip back to their hometown in central Oregon.

Every Valentine's Day after that, the balloon would mysteriously reappear, suspended from their living room balcony. Willy would change the date, but the inscription remained the same.

Then in 1999, Willy began a losing battle with cancer. One day, after a particularly difficult round of chemo, Willy took Grace's hand in his.

"Grace, as long as the air is still in that balloon, put it up every year on Valentine's Day. I blew it up with my own breath, so when you hang it up, remember that my love is still with you."

Willie passed away in December the following winter. While still devastated by the loss of her soul mate, Grace hung up the balloon on Valentine's Day, taking comfort from the unique reminder of her Willy's love.

"It's still Willy's breath in there, after all these years," says Grace with quiet amazement. "That means so much to me."

My Husband, My Love

You are my husband.
My feet shall run because of you.
My feet dance because of you.
My heart shall beat because of you.
My eyes see because of you.
My mind thinks because of you.
And I shall love because of you.

ESKIMO LOVE SONG

NO SCORECARD

MARGUERITE MURER

As the movie came to an end, the room filled with chatter. The warm fire, twinkling Christmas lights, and laughter from family brought a contented smile to my face. The minute Mom said, "Who wants…" the room emptied quicker than the stands at a losing football game.

My boyfriend, Todd, and I were the only ones left. With a bewildered look on his face, he asked me what had just happened. Catching the laughter on my mom's face, I said to Todd, "We are going to put gas in my mom's car."

He quickly replied, "It's freezing out there, and it's almost eleven-thirty."

Smiling, I said, "Then you had better put on your coat and gloves."

After hurriedly chipping the frost off the windshield, we bundled into the car. On the way to the gas station, Todd asked me to explain why in the world we were going to get my mom gas so late at night. Chuckling, I said, "When my siblings and I come home for the holidays, we help my dad get gas for my mom. It has turned into a game with all of us. We can tell when my mom is going to ask, and the last one in the room has to go."

"You have got to be kidding me!" Todd responded.

"There is no getting out of it," I said.

While pumping the gas, we clapped our hands and jumped around to stay warm. "I still don't get it. Why doesn't your mom put the gas in the car herself?" Todd asked.

With mirth in my eyes, I said, "I know it sounds insane, but let me explain. My mom has not pumped gas in over two decades. My dad always pumps gas for her." With a confused look, Todd asked if my dad was ever annoyed with having to pump gas for his wife all the time. Shaking my head, I simply said, "No, he has never complained."

"That's crazy," Todd quickly replied.

"No, not really," I explained patiently. "When I came home for the holidays my sophomore year of college, I thought I knew everything. I was on this big female independence kick. One evening, my mom and I were wrapping presents, and I told her that when I got married, my husband was going to help clean, do laundry, cook, the whole bit. Then I asked her if she ever got tired of doing the laundry and dishes. She calmly told me it did not bother her. This was difficult for me to believe. I began to give her a lecture about this being the nineties and equality between the sexes.

"Mom listened patiently. Then after setting the ribbon aside, she looked me square in the eyes. 'Someday, dear, you will understand.'

"This only irritated me more. I didn't understand one bit. And so I demanded more of an explanation. Mom smiled, and began to explain:

"'In a marriage, there are some things you like to do and some things you don't. So, together, you figure out what little things you are willing to do for each other. You share the responsibilities. I really don't mind doing the laundry. Sure, it takes some time, but it is something I do for your dad. On the other hand, I do not like to pump gas. The smell of the fumes bothers me. And I don't like to stand out in the freezing cold. So, your dad always puts gas in my car. Your dad grocery shops, and I cook. Your dad mows the grass, and I clean. I could go on and on.

"'You see,' my mother continued, 'in marriage, there is no scorecard. You do little things for each other to make the other's life easier. If you think of it as helping the person you love, you don't become annoyed with doing the laundry or cooking or any task, because you're doing it out of love.'

"Over the years, I have often reflected on what my mom said. She has a great perspective on marriage. I like how my mom and dad take care of each other. And you know what? One day, when I'm married, I don't want to have a scorecard either."

Todd was unusually quiet the rest of the way home. After he shut off the engine, he turned to me and took my hands in his with a warm smile and a twinkle in his eye.

"Anytime you want," he said in a soft voice, "I'll pump gas for you."

Love isn't love till you give it away.

OSCAR HAMMERSTEIN

THE TREASURED RING

ROCHELLE M. PENNINGTON

My mother tells the true story of the most beautiful wedding ring she has ever seen. She shared it with me shortly before my engagement when she noticed my enchantment with jewelry stores showcasing large diamonds in beautiful settings.

Her story was about an old nail wrapped around the finger of an eighty-nine-year-old lady she had met. Little would one know that this woman and her husband had become millionaires after a long life of farming in rural Iowa.

Despite the material riches which came in later years, the woman never took off her treasured little ring, even though she could have. It remained on her finger to remind her of the utmost poverty she and her husband experienced together and endured in the early years of their marriage. When love, and a little nail, was all her future husband could offer her, love and a little nail were enough.

The "gold" missing from her finger spilled out all around her—gold in the corn husks growing outside their farmhouse, gold in the hair on her husband's arms which held her close, gold in the amber of her babies' eyes. Her ring reminded her that she was rich before she had money.

The little nail, sixty-two anniversaries later, spoke of commitment. There it was on her hand—still there, always there.

And it was enough.

DO YOU WANT ME?

PARK YORK

I rise early on this Friday, as I do every day, to prepare coffee and mix a protein shake. The television news plays quietly in the corner. Flossie, my wife, is still asleep.

Sometime after eight, she begins floating out of slumber. I bring the shake to her bedside, put the straw in her mouth, and give her cheek a little pat as she begins to drink. Slowly the liquid recedes.

I sit there holding the glass, thinking about the past eight years. At first, she asked only an occasional incoherent or irrelevant question; otherwise, she was normal. I tried for two years to find out what was wrong. She was agitated, restless, defensive; she was constantly tired and unable to hold a conversation.

At last a neurologist diagnosed Alzheimer's disease. He said he wasn't sure—a firm diagnosis could come only from examining brain tissue after death. There is no known cause for this malady. And no known cure.

I enrolled Flossie in a day care center for adults. But she kept wandering off the property. We medicated her to keep her calm. Perhaps from receiving too much of one drug, she suffered a violent seizure that left her immeasurably worse: lethargic, incontinent, and unable to speak clearly or care for herself. My anguish gradually became resignation. I gave up all plans of retirement, travel, recreation, visits to see grandchildren—the golden era older people dream about.

The years have passed, and my days have become routine, demanding, lonely, seemingly without accomplishment to measure. Flossie has gradually dropped in strength and weight from one hundred twenty-five pounds to eighty-six. I take some time to work with a support group and to attend church, but the daily needs keep me feeding, bathing, diapering, changing beds, cleaning house, fixing meals, dressing and undressing her, and doing whatever else a nurse and homemaker does, morning to night.

Occasionally, a word bubbles up from the muddled processes of Flossie's diseased brain. Sometimes relevant, sometimes the name of a family member, or the name of an object. Just a single word.

On this Friday morning, after she finishes her shake, I give her some apple juice, then massage her arms and caress her forehead and cheeks. Most of the time her eyes are closed, but today she looks up at me, and suddenly her mouth forms four words in a row.

"Do you want me?"

Perfect enunciation, softly spoken. I want to jump for joy. "Of course I want you, Flossie!" I say, hugging and kissing her.

And so, after months of total silence, she has put together the most sincere question a human being can ask. She speaks, in a way, for people everywhere: those shackled by sin, addiction, hunger, thirst, mental illness, physical pain—frightened, enervated people afraid of the answer, but desperate enough to frame the question anyway.

And, Flossie, I can answer you even more specifically. It may be difficult for you to understand what's happening. That's why I'm here, to minister God's love to you, to bring you wholeness, comfort, and release. Mine are the hands God uses to do His work, just as He uses others' hands in other places. In spite of our shortcomings, we strive to make people free, well, and happy, blessing them with hope for the future while bringing protein shakes every morning.

Potpourri

❧

FRAGRANT MEDLEY

Petals and rosebuds
fragrant pastels
oils and spices
delightfully tell
there is joy in assortment
all mixed into one
like a life full of friends, family, and fun.

KIMBER ANNIE ENGSTROM

MY MOST UNFORGETTABLE FARE

KENT NERBURN

FROM *MAKE ME AN INSTRUMENT OF YOUR PEACE*

wenty years ago, I drove a cab for a living. It was a cowboy's life, a life for someone who wanted no boss. What I didn't realize was that it was also a ministry. Because I drove the night shift, my cab became a moving confessional. Passengers climbed in, sat behind me in total anonymity, and told me about their lives. I encountered people whose lives amazed me, ennobled me, made me laugh and weep. But none touched me more than a woman I picked up late one August night. I responded to a call from a small brick four-plex in a quiet part of town.

I assumed I was being sent to pick up some partyers, or someone who had just had a fight with a lover, or a worker heading to an early shift at some factory in the industrial part of town. When I arrived at 2:30 A.M., the building was dark except for a single light in a ground floor window. Under these circumstances, many drivers would just honk once or twice, wait a minute, then drive away. But I had seen too many impoverished people who depended on taxis as their only means of transportation.

Unless a situation smelled of danger, I always went to the door. This passenger might be someone who needed my assistance, I reasoned to myself. So I walked to the door and knocked. "Just a minute," answered a frail, elderly voice. I could hear something being dragged across the floor.

After a long pause, the door opened. A small woman in her eighties stood before me. She was wearing a print dress and a pillbox hat with a veil pinned on it, like somebody out of a 1940s movie. By her side was a small nylon suitcase. The apartment looked as if no one had lived in it for years. All the furniture was covered with sheets. There were no clocks on the walls, no knickknacks or utensils on the counters. In the corner was a cardboard box filled with photos and glassware. "Would you carry my bag out to the car?" she said. I took the suitcase to the cab, then returned to assist the woman. She took my arm and we walked slowly toward the curb.

She kept thanking me for my kindness. "It's nothing," I told her. "I just try to treat my passengers the way I would want my mother treated."

"Oh, you're such a good boy," she said. When we got in the cab, she gave me an address, then asked, "Could you drive through downtown?"

"It's not the shortest way," I answered quickly.

"Oh, I don't mind," she said. "I'm in no hurry. I'm on my way to a hospice." I looked in the rearview mirror. Her eyes were glistening. "I don't have any family left," she continued. "The doctor says I don't have very long." I quietly reached over and shut off the meter.

"What route would you like me to take?" I asked. For the next two hours, we drove through the city. She showed me the building where she had once worked as an elevator operator. We drove through the neighborhood where she and her husband had lived when they were newlyweds.

She had me pull up in front of a furniture warehouse that had once been a ballroom where she had gone dancing as a girl. Sometimes she'd ask me to slow in front of a particular building or corner and would sit staring into the darkness, saying nothing. As the first hint of sun was creasing the horizon, she suddenly said, "I'm tired. Let's go now." We drove in silence to the address she had given me. It was a low building, like a small convalescent home, with a driveway that passed under a portico.

Two orderlies came out to the cab as soon as we pulled up. They were solicitous and intent, watching her every move. They must have been expecting her. I opened the trunk and took the small suitcase to the door.

The woman was already seated in a wheelchair. "How much do I owe you?" she asked, reaching into her purse.

"Nothing," I said.

"You have to make a living," she answered.

"There are other passengers," I responded. Almost without thinking, I bent and gave her a hug. She held onto me tightly.

"You gave an old woman a little moment of joy," she said. "Thank you." I squeezed her hand, then walked into the dim morning light. Behind me, a door shut. It was the sound of the closing of a life.

I didn't pick up any more passengers that shift. I drove aimlessly, lost in thought. For the rest of that day, I could hardly talk. What if that woman had gotten an angry driver, or one who was impatient to end his shift? What if I had refused to take the run, or had honked once, then driven away? On a quick review, I don't think that I have done very many more important things in my life.

We're conditioned to think that our lives revolve around great moments. But great moments often catch us unaware—beautifully wrapped in what others may consider small ones.

THANK YOU, FOZZY!

RUSTY FISCHER

She was a horrible waitress. Never got anybody's order right. Always messed something up on the customers' bills so that they had to complain to the manager. There were stains all over her gaudy pink uniform and runs in her stockings, and her bright red, frizzy hair and the long, bumpy nose planted right in the middle of her oval face made her look just like that lovable muppet: Fozzy the Bear. Only, our Fozzy wasn't quite so lovable.

Or so I thought…

It was Thanksgiving night and no one else wanted to work, so it was just Fozzy and me slinging turkey shavings and ice cream scoops of mashed potatoes to the clusters of senior citizens who stumbled in out of the brisk November cold.

We had never talked much, and tonight was no exception. The diner had already started in with the Christmas carols on the Muzak, and Fozzy sang right along all night. I tried to share her enthusiasm, but I had troubles of my own.

My father's business was in disarray, and he was considering bankruptcy. After their divorce, my mother had moved to an oceanfront condominium way beyond her means. It had been for sale for a year, and no one had even attempted a bite at her ludicrous asking price.

My life felt out of control, and I had no one to turn to. With so many troubles of their own, how could I politely remind my parents that they had always offered to help pay for my college tuition. I had been slaving away at the diner for nearly a year now, trying to save up enough for my first semester at the local state university. I was almost there, and then just this morning, my car hadn't started. I soon learned that the entire electrical system was faulty. It would cost over five hundred dollars to fix.

"Five hundred dollars?" I heard someone respond. I blinked my eyes and stared into Fozzy's solemn face. "And just when you were so close to starting college, too. Not a very happy Thanksgiving, is it?"

Had I really said all of my troubles out loud? And had Fozzy actually listened?

But there we were, nestled quietly over two cups of mudlike diner coffee as the last few customers of the evening wandered out into the miserable cold.

"Thank you," I said humbly, feeling a lump in my throat at having judged Fozzy so badly. "Thank you for listening. I didn't mean to go on like that."

"Well, now," she sighed. "It doesn't sound like there's much listening going on in your house these days. Everybody rushing around with their own problems. Sometimes a friendly ear can change the way you think about things." She was right. Pouring out my troubles, things I hadn't even told my best friends for fear of embarrassment, had left me feeling like I'd just had a restful night's sleep.

"Listen," she said as we finished our side work and clocked out. "I've been trying to sell my old car for weeks. It's in good shape. Now, it's not exactly a babe magnet, but I'm only asking three hundred dollars for it. That's less than it would take to fix your car. Maybe the money you save would round out what you need for tuition."

"And then some," I gasped, leaping at the offer like a little kid. We sat quietly on the way to her apartment, the only two on the bus. Everyone else was busy celebrating the holiday with family and friends. I thought of my mom at her annual gala Thanksgiving dinner party at the country club. And my dad working doubletime at his company to try and make things right. Neither of them had even bothered to ask me what I'd be doing for the holiday.

Fozzy's car was an eleven-year-old Honda with just a little rust and nearly new tires. Its paint job was faded and the interior was worn, but it turned over in an instant and purred like a kitten. There were over one hundred thousand miles on it, but it was in better shape than the car I was planning on having fixed. I couldn't believe my good luck.

"The paperwork's upstairs," said Fozzy. "You wait here and I'll go get it. I'm sure you have big plans for tonight. I wouldn't want to keep you."

I watched sadly as Fozzy's ample backside waddled slowly away from me. She favored one leg, and the soles of her dollar store shoes looked old and worn. The halls of her building were dark and quiet, and I had picked up enough clues so far to determine that Fozzy wasn't exactly walking into a festive apartment tonight either.

It didn't take long to catch up to her. Her smile filled the corridor as we opened her door, and she fumbled through a cheap desk for the car's paperwork. I sat on a threadbare couch and looked around her one bedroom apartment while she searched. The room was clean and cozy. The table was set with a paper tablecloth bearing turkeys and pilgrims. Turkey candles and pilgrim saltshakers rounded out her festive holiday decorations.

"Oh, I'm sorry," I said, seeing the table set for two and getting up. "I didn't realize you were expecting company."

Fozzy smiled sadly, looking at her feeble attempts to bring the holidays into her home. "Oh no," she sighed. "That's just habit. Ever since my husband died six years ago, I can't stand to see a table set for one. I just leave two plates out so people don't go feeling sorry for me.

"I don't even know why I bothered this year," she added, handing me the car's title as I wrote her a check for three hundred dollars. "You don't need to set a table for take-out Chinese food."

I looked around the room at the shabby furniture and homemade curtains. Scattered about were photographs of several young men and women in various celebratory poses: graduations, promotions, and birthdays. Younger versions of Fozzy were standing nearby, smiling proudly.

Where were her own children this holiday night?

Just then my stomach rumbled. I'd been too upset all night to even think about food. Now I was suddenly starving.

"Listen," I said, pulling out the wad of ones and fives from my shift at the diner. "I had a pretty good night. Why don't I order us up some take-out so your nice table here doesn't go to waste? My treat. It's the least I can do to thank you for bailing me out like this."

Fozzy couldn't find the phone fast enough.

Later, as Fozzy showed off the interior of the car and its impressive features, most of which no longer worked, I noticed the stains on her uniform and felt an aching in my heart. Her kind and generous gesture had afforded me the opportunity to finally start college on time. Classes would start soon; I would move away from home and, once settled, find a cushy job on campus and start the process of financial aid and student loans.

My long, hard nights of dishing up buttered carrots and creamed spinach were nearly at an end. I wondered how many long, hard years Fozzy would have to work before she could finally retire.

Driving away in my new used car, toward a bright future thanks to the kind acts of a near stranger, I ran over a bump and the faulty glove box door swung open. Inside was a thin envelope. I opened it at a stoplight and then pulled over until my tears dried up and I could see the road again.

"Thank you for the first Thanksgiving I've celebrated in six years," said a quickly scrawled note on cheap stationery. "This isn't much, but it's all the tips I made tonight. Maybe you can buy one of your textbooks on me. Thanks again, Mavis."

"Mavis," I thought, finally pulling back onto the road. All those nights together and it was sitting right there on her name tag the whole time: "Mavis." I counted the money in the envelope. There was enough for two textbooks, but there was also just enough for a brand new uniform for Mavis. I couldn't wait to give it to her the next night.

THE PEACEKEEPER

GLORIA CASSITY STARGEL

*T*he day our younger son, Rick, left home for the Marine Corps was a heart-wrenching one for me. Besides the fact that I just hate good-byes, this was my "baby" going off to become a fighting man. I couldn't help worrying that military training would destroy Rick's loving, compassionate spirit. *Dear Lord, make him tough, if necessary. But please, Lord,* I prayed, *keep him tender.* Now who but a mother would make a request like that?

Rick endured the rigors of basic training and Officer Candidate School. Then, after advanced instruction, he was assigned to the Marine Corps Air Station in Cherry Point, North Carolina. There, seeking a little off-duty peace and quiet of his own, he rented a small house out in the country. Always athletic—baseball, football, weight lifting, waterskiing, tennis—he looked forward to the solitude of his daily six-mile run along picturesque fields and meadows.

A problem developed, though. It seemed that each farm had several dogs. They didn't take too kindly to this strange intruder racing through their territories. Every day, by the time Rick made it back to his house, he was tripping over a whole pack of yelping dogs, most of them snarling at his heels. It was *not* the tranquil time he had envisioned. Hoping to discourage the attackers, he tried kicking, swinging a stick, yelling. Nothing worked.

One day, Rick phoned home. "Mother," he began, "you know those dogs that have been making my life miserable? Well, I remembered you taught us 'kindness always pays,' so I decided to give it a try."

"What did you do?" I asked.

"Yesterday as I ran," he said, "when my patience had been pushed to the limit, I just stopped in my tracks, whirled around to face them, stooped down on one knee, and talked to them in my best 'pet talk' voice. And you know what?" Rick's voice was smiling now. "Those dogs started wagging their tails and kissing me on the face, each trying to get closer than the other."

"What happened when you ran?" I wanted to know.

"You wouldn't believe the difference," Rick said. "It was *so* peaceful! Passing one farm after the other, the whole crowd fell in and ran as usual. But this time they ran *with* me—not against me. I must have looked like the Pied Piper by the time we got back to my house."

I smiled into the phone, picturing my young, still-sensitive son. Rick had solved his problem. And God had answered a mother's prayer.

Each day comes bearing its own gifts.
Untie the ribbons.

RUTH ANN SCHABACKER

YUK IT UP!

❧

PATSY CLAIRMONT
FROM NORMAL IS JUST A SETTING ON YOUR DRYER

*W*e all have moments we'd rather not remember—
the kind that when we do recall them, we get
embarrassed all over again. Like finding you're dragging a long sweep of toilet tissue. Spike heels are great for that. You shish kebab the tissue on your way out of the restroom, and you can literally parade it for miles before anyone will tell you.

Having dragged my pantyhose behind me through my hometown has left me with empathy for other dragees. I remember a gentleman and his wife who approached me at a convention and related their adventure.

The man said, "If you think it's embarrassing for a woman to drag her pantyhose, how do you think a man feels when it happens to him? I went to work and walked through the office when one of the women sang out, 'What's that, Bill?' I turned to look, and dangling out of my suit-pants leg were my wife's pantyhose. I casually ambled over to a wall, shook them out, and walked away. I left the hose huddled in the corner to figure out their own transportation home."

Evidently his wife didn't pick up her pantyhose, but the static in his slacks did. Half the hose clung to his pant leg, while the remaining leg danced behind him. The man, his wife, and I laughed long and loud as he relived his tale.

There's something so healing about laughter. When I can laugh at an event that has the potential to turn my pale face flashing red, somehow the situation doesn't record itself in my memory with as much pain.

My friend Ann is a good example. She flipped her melon and lived to laugh about it. While she was shopping for groceries one time, she spotted a large, elongated watermelon. She wanted the melon, but it looked heavy, and she wasn't sure she could lift it. No stock boys were around, so she decided to give it the old heave-ho. Either the melon didn't weigh as much as she had thought, or she was stronger than she realized. Anyway, she grabbed hold of the watermelon and slung it up and toward herself. With torpedo speed, the slippery melon slid out of her hands and up her shoulder to become airborne.

Once again, Sir Newton's theory of gravitation proved true. The melon headed for earth with great rapidity. When a melon is dropped from more than five feet onto a tile floor, "splat" doesn't begin to describe what occurs. Not only did it explode, but everything in a fifteen-foot radius was affected as well.

As Ann turned to look at her Herculean effort gone awry, she spotted...a victim. Or should I say the victim was "spotted"? A nicely dressed businesswoman looked stunned as ragged chunks of watermelon dripped down her pantyhose.

Ann didn't mean to laugh, but the whole scene struck her as so absurd that she couldn't help herself. The lady was not laughing, which seemed to tickle Ann all the more. The woman marched off in a huff, leaving a trail of seeds behind her.

Ann was now leaning against the rutabagas, trying to catch her breath, when the manager walked up and said, "This is not funny."

Well, that was the wrong thing to say. Poor Ann howled. Her sides were splitting, her face was red, and she was hysterical. She said she was trying to gain her composure so she could find the lady to apologize to her. But finally she had to just leave the store.

Laughter can make moments more memorable. Whether laughing alone or with others, it helps us feel good about our memories.

I remember walking through the mall once when I noticed a quarter on the floor. Had it been a penny, I might have passed it by. But a quarter? No way. I stooped down and swooped my hand across the floor to scoop up the coin, but it didn't budge. I tried again. I could hear laughter coming from a nearby ice cream shop, but I didn't look because I was focused on the shiny coin. I tried to pick it up again, but it held fast. I tried prying it with my nails. I even took out my emery board and used it like a crowbar, trying to dislodge this gleaming coin. As I stared at George Washington's immobile silhouette, I thought I saw him smirk. Then I realized George was not alone. The laughter nearby had grown to unbridled guffawing. I looked up and realized five teenagers were watching me and laughing at my financial struggle. It was the kind of laugh that told me they knew something I didn't. I could have flown off in a flurry or resented their intrusion. Then again, I could find out what was so hilarious and join the fun.

I asked, "Okay, so what's the deal?"

One girl confessed they had glued the quarter to the floor and had been watching people try to pick it up. The kids dubbed me the "most dedicated to the task." I giggled with them as I thought about my twenty-five-cent antics.

Laughter is an incredible gift. It helps us not to take ourselves too seriously and makes it possible for us to survive life's awkward moments.

FOR HIS EYES ONLY

KATHLEEN RUCKMAN

I remember the Christmas she left a card for our family on the table and signed it, "The Cleaning Lady." Even though we'd known her for years, Heather didn't sign her name.

Unassuming, yet filled with quiet strength, Heather rides her bicycle to the houses she cleans. I've seen her pedaling her bike, the basket filled with cleaning supplies, through all parts of town.

And in all types of weather.

One winter we had an ice storm. The whole town turned to shimmering glass—even the tiny tree branches. I'd called Heather that morning, telling her not to come. But she came anyway, braving the sleet and icy roads, greeting me with red-rosy cheeks.

"Oh, you do what you have to do," she simply said.

Heather would never accept rides back home, even when I offered again and again. On the days it poured down rain, her yellow hooded raincoat was all she needed. It relieved me to know she would be more visible in traffic when she rode in bad weather.

Heather's life inspired me.

Heather's husband did lawn jobs in the summer and odd jobs during the winter. I once saw him ringing the Salvation Army bell at Christmas.

He and Heather take in at least one homeless person at a time. There's rarely a day when they don't have someone extra living with them.

I asked Heather once how they managed. "How do you get by with taking in so many people without a break?"

Not wanting to make a big deal of it, Heather stopped dusting and said in a soft voice, "Oh, it all works out. When one person leaves, it seems the Lord sends another." Explanation done, she returned to her work.

Heather is so shy that it's difficult for her to make eye contact with others. Over the years, I've tried to make conversation with her, but she works as she speaks, never stopping to chat. She puts her energy into her work: scrubbing, wiping, doing windows, and even stacking firewood.

Several years ago, I left for the day and let Heather know I'd be gone all afternoon. I left her a check on the kitchen counter with a note saying I'd see her in two weeks.

But I returned home that day, earlier than either of us had expected.

I opened the front door quietly, not wanting to startle Heather. I stepped into the foyer, then froze in thrilled silence as the strains of praise songs drifted down from upstairs.

Could this be our quiet Heather? The strong, smooth voice coming from above was filled with beauty and passion. Her lovely voice reminded me of professional opera singers I'd heard recently at our Performing Arts center.

I stood there for a few moments, listening. Then my heart melted as I realized that Heather *was* performing—for an audience of One.

I slipped out the front door, careful not to give myself away. As far as she knew, only her God had heard her sing. As I drove away, a quiet awe filled my soul. I thought of the buttercups, wild roses, and other wildflowers that grace the lonely hills, offering up a silent symphony to their Creator. Unnoticed by the world, these humble flowers bring pleasure to the Father's heart alone.

Some things, I realized, are for His eyes only.

LONG-TERM ROMANCE

Ruth Bell Graham
from *It's My Turn*

other had had a stroke several years before which had left her confined to a wheelchair, with her speech slightly affected. Frequently Daddy was up at four in the morning to have his Bible study and time of prayer so he could devote the rest of his day to Mother.

I stood by to help in any way I could, often taking the evening meal down to them and bringing Mother up to stay with me when Daddy would have to be gone for several days.

One morning when I dropped by to see how they were, I found Daddy on his knees in front of Mother, helping her put on her stockings.

Daddy had reached the point where he got up and down with difficulty. He, who had been an athlete in his younger days, and had always kept himself in top physical shape, now found himself with a painfully ulcerated toe that refused to heal due to the fact that he was a borderline diabetic and had lost circulation in his left leg.

He glanced up at me over his glasses, giving me his usual broad smile of welcome.

"You know," he said, returning to Mother's stocking, "these are the happiest days of our lives. Caring for your mother is the greatest privilege of my life."

And the nice thing was, he meant it.

FINDING MY WAY HOME

KAY MARSHALL STROM

Our family was vacationing in England when we got news that wildfires were roaring through Santa Barbara. Within six hours we got the telephone call we had been dreading: "Your house has burned. Everything is gone."

Everything? All our family pictures? My daughter's art portfolio? My grandfather's Bible where we kept the records of all the births and deaths of generations of our family? The silverware my husband's grandmother had carried with her all the way from Sweden? *Everything?*

I hung up the phone, and my husband and children and I stared at each other in shocked silence.

My husband, Larry, was showing unmistakable signs of a serious illness and my children were ready to go away to college, so the trip to England was to be our last family vacation together. It had been wonderful. But now this.

That evening we all sat around a small table in our room and took all the photos out of our wallets. Carefully, tenderly, we spread them out to see what we had left. That little pile of photographs brought back a flood of memories—times when we were all healthy and happy and our future seemed so promising. Back when I still believed I could handle anything that came my way.

As we flew home the next day, my mind was flooded with fear and confusion. If everything was gone, what was I going to do? Larry was no longer able to work. Lisa and Eric would be away at college. It was all up to me—to rebuild the house, to earn the money to support the family and pay college bills, to care for my husband. How could I ever keep our family together? I just wanted to get home…but we *had* no home to go to.

Nothing could have prepared us for what we found when we got back to Santa Barbara. Our neighborhood was devastated. Tears filled my eyes as I looked down our hill where 105 homes once stood. Now I could only count eight. Everywhere we looked we saw charred ruins, blackened chimneys, and burned-out cars.

Workmen were already there with bulldozers, waiting impatiently to clear our lot. But I couldn't let them. Not yet. Again and again I sifted through the ashes, desperate to find something I could hold in my hand, something I could carry away with me, something that would give me a link to the past. But there was nothing. And the workmen were getting more and more impatient.

Finally I had no choice—there was nothing to do but give up and walk away.

As I stumbled through the rubble that had been my home, my foot hit against something buried deep in the ashes. I bent down and dug it out, then I blew off the dust and ashes.

In my hand I held the most amazing thing. Glistening in the sun, it resembled a piece of modern art. At the center were turkey-shaped salt and pepper shakers forged together beak-to-beak. My school teacher gave them to me when I was twelve years old. She was the person who had always believed in me, the one who told me that someday I would be a writer. On top of them was the base of a silver candlestick, a precious wedding gift. Cemented to its side were the melted remains of a cup and saucer Larry had bought me on our honeymoon. On the other side was the smooth, shiny white of my grandmother's milk glass sugar bowl. In one corner was a locket I was given for my high school graduation. Firmly affixed to the left side were the fork and spoon Lisa used when she first started feeding herself. On the other side was Eric's long-handled baby spoon. The entire sculpture was glazed over with what had been our collection of crystal goblets.

It was a piece of art from the hand of God! He had left me a summary of my life I could hold in my hand. He had preserved a piece of our home.

Our house was gone. Where we once ate and slept, practiced the piano and baked cookies, played games and opened Christmas gifts, nothing remained but a bare dirt lot. But our home? That we would carry with us in our hearts forever.

A Perfect Rose

Dressed in worn and faded, ragged clothes,
in her wilted hand one ruby rose.
She bears her precious treasure with such care,
that people pause to glance, and some to stare.
Was it stolen from the city park—
taken late at night when it was dark?
Surely, this old woman couldn't grow
such a rose as this, you all must know.
The woman makes her way across the street,
to the corner where the sad ones meet.
She stops and looks into the stranger's eyes
then with a smile, she gives the girl the prize.
The girl lights up as if she understands,
she cups the bright red
flower in both hands.
And God looks down and
smiles because He knows
this ragged woman is
His perfect Rose.

MELODY CARLSON
FROM WOMEN ARE SISTERS AT HEART

IN A HURRY

GINA BARRETT SCHLESINGER

I came rushing through our dining room in my best suit, focused on getting ready for an evening meeting. Gillian, my four-year-old, was dancing about to one of her favorite oldies, "Cool," from *West Side Story*.

I was in a hurry, on the verge of being late. Yet a small voice inside of me said, "Stop."

So I stopped. I looked at her. I reached out, grabbed her hand, and spun her around. My seven-year-old, Caitlin, came into our orbit, and I grabbed her, too. The three of us did a wild jitterbug around the dining room and into the living room. We were laughing. We were spinning. Could the neighbors see the lunacy through the windows? It didn't matter. The song ended with a dramatic flourish and our dance finished with it. I patted them on their bottoms and sent them to take their baths.

They went up the stairs, gasping for breath, their giggles bouncing off the walls. I went back to business. I was bent over, shoving papers into my briefcase, when I overheard my youngest say to her sister, "Caitlin, isn't Mommy the bestest one?"

I froze. How close I had come to hurrying through life, missing that moment. My mind went to the awards and diplomas that covered the walls of my office. No award, no achievement I have ever earned can match this: "Isn't Mommy the bestest one?"

My child said that at age four. I don't expect her to say it at age fourteen. But at age forty, if she bends down over that pine box to say goodbye to the cast-off container of my soul, I want her to say it then.

"Isn't Mommy the bestest one?"

It doesn't fit on my resume. But I want it on my tombstone.

SPECIAL DELIVERY

RICHARD FLANAGAN

This past spring my wife passed away after a six-month battle with colon cancer.

She spent two months, last November and December, in a convalescent home. I visited her every day and watched her condition change from bad to worse, although some days she would rally and seem to have a very good day. Her spirits rarely faltered as she maintained a cheerful outlook and seldom, if ever, complained about anything.

Each day, she had a request for some food that she had a craving for. Those cravings ranged from all varieties of fruit to pizza. On my visits, I always brought what she had requested. She always had me help her with her laps, which consisted of her walking from her hospital bed to one end of the hospital corridor and back, once, twice, and even three times on a good day.

You see, she thought, and I hoped, that she would beat this terrible disease. After New Year's, I brought her home and she was very happy being in her own bed. On the twelfth of February, she quietly slipped away, with my daughter, a few close family members, and me at her bedside.

Now with the holidays fast approaching, my thoughts often turn to holiday celebrations of the past, and my daughter frequently asks me what we are going to do without Mom here.

The doorbell rang recently, and as I answered the door the postman greeted me. He handed me a letter. It was marked "Special Delivery" and as I read the return address, I saw that it was from the convalescent home where my wife had stayed. I signed for the letter and thought to myself it was nice of someone from the home to remember us at this time of year.

There are no words to explain my elation as I took out the folded pages from the envelope and began to read the first page.

Thanksgiving, 1999

To My Beloved Family,

I do not know if I will be with you next Thanksgiving or not, but please know that my spirit and my heart will be with you.

I am reminded this day of all the wonderful holidays that we had together over the years. Every one was a precious day to me, especially thinking about them now. The two of you must be strong, and I am sure that you will be.

Richard, I hope that you decorate the table gaily with a nice tablecloth, fine linen place mats, and our best china and silverware. Remember the two silver candleholders you gave me on our twenty-fifth anniversary? You could use those as a centerpiece and maybe you and Tricia could each light one candle as you say what you are thankful for.

Look in the big Betty Crocker cookbook. Near the pages on how to prepare a turkey for baking, you will find my grandmother's old recipe and also Aunt Clara's recipe for fruit salad. I am positive between you and Tricia you can put together a dinner fit for a king— and queen, which you both are.

I am writing this from my hospital bed and Karen, the charge nurse, is helping me. I told her to hold this letter for me until next Thanksgiving and then to mail it "Special Delivery."

I must stop now as tears are blurring my vision. Always know that I love you both. I know that I can be proud of you, and that you will have a wonderful day.

May God and His blessings be with you always,

Mom

*We can complain because rose bushes have thorns
or rejoice because thorn bushes have roses.*

DAG HAMMARSKJOLD

THE GRAY SLIPPER

❧

PEARL NELSON
AS TOLD TO LYNNE M. THOMPSON

*I*t's only a matter of time now," the doctors told me. Mom's eighty-three-year-old body was saying enough. I consoled myself, knowing death would provide relief from pain and usher in a whole new, wonderful experience.

Still, all I could think about was the gray slipper.

As the oldest daughter of five, and the only one who lived in the same town as Mom, caretaking responsibilities for the past ten years rested on my shoulders. Throughout the course of this slow, debilitating process, we had grown very close. Visiting doctors, finding support care, moving her into various elder care homes, as her condition worsened, made for quality time and, sometimes, humorous episodes.

Only two weeks ago my mother had been admitted to the hospital for what they believed was a cracked hip. The X rays proved negative, so she was released and sent back to the convalescent home. That night the hospital called me to report that Mom had left behind one gray slipper. Knowing I had just purchased a new pair for her, and realizing she was probably through traipsing the halls anyway, I instructed them to throw it out. While visiting my mom at the convalescent home that night, I told her about the stray slipper.

"I love those slippers; they are so cozy," she whimpered.

235

"I already told them to throw it out; besides, you have this nice new pair," I assured her.

"Go get the other one, please," Mom begged.

"I can't. It's late. I'm tired, and it's probably already on the bottom of the trash bin."

I left that night feeling a tinge of guilt, but at the same time justified in my resolve.

Tonight, however, standing beside her hospital bed again, guilt gave way to remorse. I know people often live with regrets, good-byes left unsaid, deeds left undone, but I was determined I would not befall such a fate. Now, I wished for another chance to say "I care." I care enough to give you hope, for a slipper you would never be able to wear; to give you comfort in familiar things; to give you a feeling of worth, dignity, and control, when all around you seems helpless, and your personhood stripped. I knew if given the chance again, I would not betray a trust.

The hours ticked away, and Mom drifted in and out of sleep. My stomach growled. My sister arrived and agreed to keep vigil. I kissed Mom's cheek and slipped away for a quick bite. As I sat alone in the cafeteria with my contrite conscience, I couldn't help but wonder about the people dining around me. Did they know how precious life is? That each day is a gift from God? Did they realize the opportunity they have to tenderly touch another life, leaving what might be their last impression on them?

I knew my mother would forgive me for the lost slipper; we had too much good history together. Still, I felt a shadow of regret that I acted so hastily. I finished the last of my coffee and headed back up to the room. When I walked back in, Mom was awake. She looked happy to see me.

"Oh, look," my sister said. "A policeman came in and made me sign for this; he said it belongs to Mom." I blinked in utter disbelief. It was the gray slipper.

"I don't care who you think brought that in," I told my sister. "An angel sent this to me."

"A slipper?" my sister asked. "Mom can't even walk. She doesn't need it."

"It's not for her," I said holding it to my chest. "It's for me."

THE MOST VALUABLE PLAYER

CHRISTINE REDNER

A chilly March day gave way to a frigid evening as the eight-year-old stepped up to the plate in the batter's box. It was Holly's first time playing softball, and as I watched from my perch on the metal bleachers with the other parents, I shivered and hugged the blanket a little tighter. This was just a "scrimmage," a practice game that didn't officially count on the scorebooks, but I was certain Holly would demonstrate the same athletic prowess that blessed her older brother, Ryan. Holly's long hair hung down her back from a ponytail stuck through the hole in the back of her brother's worn baseball cap, and she proudly wore the new softball glove he gave her for Christmas. Finally, after all the years of standing on the sidelines watching Ryan play ball, this was Holly's time to shine.

Her face was a study in determination as she waited for the first pitch. I held my breath as she swung with all her might at the ball. Strike one. Holly stood a little straighter and stuck out her chin, readying herself for the next pitch. Strike two. I dug my fingernails into my palms as I clenched my fists beneath the blanket and willed the ball to connect with the bat. Holly simply smiled and tossed her ponytail, then steeled herself once more for the task at hand. Along came the pitch, a mighty swing…and strike three.

Four times Holly was up to bat that game, and each attempt produced the same results. Although I grew more and more impatient and edgy, Holly's attitude was much different. She approached the batter's box as a warrior heading out to battle, her head high, her steps determined, her slender form poised. Each time she struck out, she smiled and waved at me as she sat back down on the bench in the dugout.

In spite of Holly's lackluster softball skills, the game was close, and I began to relax a little and just watch her play. Holly's enthusiasm never dimmed. She jumped up and down in the outfield when her teammates made a great play, her arms stretched toward the sky, fists balled in victory as she shouted encouragement. She did a little dance and ran off the field when each inning was over and it was finally their turn to bat again. She bounced like a kangaroo and hugged her teammates as they came to the dugout after having scored a run.

When it was finally over, Holly's team lost by a score of twelve to ten. As I gathered my belongings together and unfolded my tense, stiff body from the bleachers, I tried to think of something appropriately "motherly" and consoling to say to my daughter, whom I was certain would be heartbroken.

As I walked toward the field, Holly ran toward me, wrapping her arms around me in a giant hug. "Mom!" she shouted with glee. "We almost won!"

I started to laugh as my daughter's wisdom began to sink in. The game wasn't about winning; it was just about playing and having a good time. "You sure did, honey," was all I could say. "I'm so proud of you!" And I was. By her positive outlook, Holly reminded me how games should be played, how work should be tackled, and how life should be lived. And in an instant, Holly became The Most Valuable Player to me.

PRECIOUS CARGO

LAURIE PATTERSON

When I put our daughter on the school bus that beautiful, sunny day last week, I couldn't have known the chain of events that would follow. The day started like any other. As the bus pulled away from our driveway, I waved good-bye and headed back inside to begin my workday.

I could see that storm clouds were brewing in the distance—rolling in from Lake Erie. There was nothing unusual about that. While western New Yorkers probably enjoy some of the most beautiful summers anywhere, we also prepare ourselves for some pretty rough winters. Most of us think the snow is beautiful, and easier to cope with than hurricanes, floods, tornadoes, and mudslides. Snow is not an impediment—we carry on with our business without giving it much thought. Our local governments are well prepared for this type of weather…usually.

However, no one could have predicted what would happen. Although snow was forecast, no one expected anything of this magnitude. Not even the television weathermen, especially not this early in the season. I got my first inkling of disaster midafternoon, when weather reports began to pour in and it became clear that Mother Nature was unleashing the landlocked version of "the perfect storm."

A quick phone call to the school district bus garage and the rumor was confirmed—our daughter's bus was just twenty miles to our north—where the ravaging storm was packing its most powerful punch. She was on her way home, but with thousands of motorists gridlocked and abandoning their vehicles on the road to seek shelter, could they make it? Their normal route home, on the highway, was impassable.

At that point, all of our prayers and hopes were with one person—Flo Russell, one of the most dedicated people we know—and the person behind the wheel of our daughter's bus. She, and her assistant, Sue Shults, were charged with the safety of not only our daughter, but that of twins and another young special needs boy. What would they do? How would they be able to protect them?

If there was anyone in this world whom we could entrust with that precious cargo, it would be Flo. We've known her for five years, and her son frequently visits our home to play with our boys. She is friendly and outgoing, and we've been fortunate to have her as our daughter's driver for the last couple of years. While others might think of her as just a bus driver, the parents of those special needs children know the truth—Flo has become a lifesaver in understanding and monitoring the condition of those kids on her bus. It's not easy and it's not simple.

The hours ticked by slowly. My husband and I made numerous phone calls to try and determine their location and relay our medical concerns. By early evening, our boys were repeatedly inquiring as to the whereabouts of their sister—three hours overdue.

Outwardly I was calm and reassuring, but I was beginning to feel fear gripping my throat. The storm had dumped over two feet of snow in a few short hours, and a state of emergency was declared. The roads were impassable, phone lines were jammed, and we all felt helpless. If the bus was trapped in that mess, there was virtually no way to evacuate those four kids. There was no way to help. They were only about twenty miles away, but they might as well have been on the other side of the planet.

Our daughter, Laura, is medically fragile. She has little vision, decreased hearing, and cannot speak. For anyone unfamiliar with her it would be nearly impossible to anticipate or interpret her needs. She is fed through a "button" in her stomach, and she needs special medication to control seizures. This situation was very serious.

Then, at 8:30 P.M. the phone rang—it was the district bus garage. Flo, in her infinite wisdom, had avoided the highways and had somehow managed to extract their bus from the gridlock and steer them to her sister's house. And her sister was a nurse!

In five hours, they had only traveled a mile or two, but the kids were safe and warm, and medical care was available if needed. They would not be coming home that night.

After doling out drinks, food, and blankets, Flo was on the phone with all of us. What medications and supplies were needed, she inquired. What special considerations did she need to know about? She gave me the phone number for the nearest pharmacy so I could make arrangements with our pediatrician to call in prescriptions.

With the kids now happily watching television and supervised by Sue, Flo stepped back out into the ferocious storm and slowly trudged through snow drifts to the pharmacy. Once there, she even requested that the pharmacist call the doctors back to ask for an additional dose or two of medications because an early morning attempt to travel home did not look promising—there was a driving ban.

Flo called us several more times that evening to report that medications had been given and all was well. She and Sue remained awake most of the night, watching over the children.

As the sun rose the next morning, Flo was again back on the phone communicating with parents, reassuring us that everyone was fine.

Their journey home resumed again at ten-thirty that morning. Even in broad daylight, with a police designed travel route, it took three and a half hours for the bus to make it to our home.

The bus rolled up our driveway with great fanfare—horn blaring and occupants cheering. Flo flipped open the bus doors and greeted me with a big smile and a hug. She had safely delivered her charges home once again.

We had many things to be thankful for on Thanksgiving—one of them was a little-known bus driver from Orchard Park, New York, whom we consider a hero—Flo Russell.

Sweet Memories

KEEPSAKES OF THE HEART

*The heart is like a treasure chest
that's filled with souvenirs.
It's there we keep the memories
we gather through the years.*

AUTHOR UNKNOWN

HIGH BUTTON SHOES

MARGARET JENSEN
FROM *THE GREATEST LESSON I'VE EVER LEARNED*

I needed shoes! I *always* needed shoes! Papa traveled throughout the province of Saskatchewan to minister to the needs of the Scandinavian immigrants, so our bank account was Philippians 4:19: "My God shall supply all your needs." He did—but not always my way!

The arrival of the "missionary barrel" was an annual event in our home. Every outdated relic from the past seemed to find its way into that barrel: moth-eaten coats, hats with plumes and feathers, corsets with the stays, threadbare silks and satins, shoes of all sizes and shapes.

Mama used the hand-me-downs from the missionary barrel to make clothes for her children. She wasted nothing. Buttons, silks, and furs were transformed into beautiful dresses and coats. The scraps were put together for pallets for the floor, or sewn into quilts. We never lacked quilts!

"Margaret," Papa called, "we have shoes!"

I started to run away. I had lived through enough missionary barrel debuts to know I probably wouldn't like the shoes Papa had found.

"I'm sure they won't fit." I kept running.

"Margaret!"

I stopped. I went to Papa and stared in horror when he held up the monstrosities—two pair of high button shoes, a black pair and a brown pair. Oxfords were "in"; button shoes were "out"!

"Try them on." Papa left no room for discussion.

I complained that they were too big.

"Ja, that is good. We'll put cotton in the toes. They'll last a long time." No one argued with Papa.

Mama sensed my distress and tenderly said, "Margaret, we prayed for shoes, and now we have shoes. Wear your shoes with a thankful and humble heart. It is not so important what you have on the feet, but it is very important where the feet go. This could be one of life's valuable lessons." (No ten-year-old is interested in "valuable lessons.")

I knew better than to argue with God and Mama on this point, but I had a plan. Papa's sermons on faith told of Moses and the crossing of the Red Sea, Daniel in the den of lions. "If you have faith, you can move mountains," Papa's voice echoed in my mind. I knew what to do.

I carefully placed the shoes (buttonhook included!) beside my bedroom door and prayed, "Oh, God, keep Your mountains, but move my shoes. Thank You."

The next morning I fully expected the shoes to be gone. Was I in for a surprise. They were still there. Something went wrong! I had a strange suspicion that it might be related to Mama's "valuable lessons."

"Hurry, Margaret," Mama called. "Time for Sunday school."

I buckled up my galoshes over those awful high button shoes and reluctantly trekked off in the snow to Sunday school. *If I can keep my galoshes on, no one will see my horrible shoes,* I thought to myself. *Tomorrow I'll think of something else.*

Upon arriving at church, I carefully wiped off my galoshes and started into class. A booming voice called out, "Margaret, no one goes into Sunday school class with galoshes on. You're dripping."

Slowly I unbuckled my galoshes, and there I stood, for all the world to see, in my embarrassing old high button shoes. My face grew hot as I felt my classmates' silent pity.

Then my friend Dorothy came in, and she was also carefully wiping off her galoshes. The same voice of authority boomed out, "Dorothy, take off your galoshes. You're dripping."

Slowly, Dorothy removed her galoshes…and stood before us in a pair of hand-knit socks. She had no shoes. There we were, two ten-year-old girls, learning life's "valuable lesson."

"Good morning, young ladies," came the crisp English accent of our beloved Sunday school teacher. Mr. Avery, a frail, elderly, blue-eyed gentleman with white hair and a goatee, quietly assessed the situation.

Each Sunday, as we formed a large circle in our class, Mr. Avery chose two children to sit beside him. It was almost like sitting next to God. This morning Mr. Avery announced, "Dorothy, you sit here on one side of me and, Margaret, you sit here on the other."

The shoes and socks were forgotten. He had picked us! Mr. Avery had picked us! My old shoes and Dorothy's socks didn't matter to Mr. Avery. He had picked us anyway! I remember very little of what he said that morning—but I'll never forget what he did.

When it was time to leave, Dorothy and I pulled on our galoshes and walked out into the snow. Our heads were held high—Mr. Avery had picked us!

Mama was right. It is not so important what is on our feet, but where our feet go.

THE CHRISTMAS ROOM

GILLETTE JONES

When I arrived at my daughter's on Christmas Eve, her children ran to the door with shouts and kisses. Then, struggling with my bags, they took me to the guest room. I stopped short at the door, staring at the sign that hung there. In red and green crayon it read, "The Christmas Room." My throat ached for a moment, as I remembered…

Our daughter Barbara was only nine when she began to realize that we were quite poor. In Barbara's class there was one girl who took special delight in tormenting her. Joan came from the wealthiest family in town, one of the few that hadn't been affected by the Great Depression.

Joan was outgoing, Barbara quiet and shy. Joan was all ups and downs: one minute befriending Barbara, treating her to candy, giving her a toy—the next, bragging extravagantly, teaching Barbara to be ashamed of our house.

We kept hoping Barbara would overcome her shyness and make other friends, but she continued to tag after Joan.

Christmas was coming. I knew ours would be a lean one indeed, unless we used a great deal of imagination. Early in November we started planning. Barbara helped me look for recipes that were inexpensive. We colored Epsom salt and put it in pretty bottles as bath salts for her grandmothers. We took scraps of velvet and transformed ordinary boxes into jewelry boxes for the grandfathers' stickpins. We dreamed up pincushions that looked like miniature hats and pot holders in the shape of teapots.

We spent hours in the little spare room laughing at each new touch of imagination. The lumpy old daybed became littered with gay scraps of paper as we cut pictures from last year's Christmas cards to decorate our packages. We had a wonderful time.

One day, Barbara went to Joan's house after school and returned looking sad.

"What's the trouble?" I asked her.

"Oh, nothing." She hesitated, then said, "Mom, I told a fib today. But that Joan! She's always talking about her guest room and the company that sleeps there. Today she asked, 'Where does your company sleep?'"

Barbara went on. "I told Joan we don't have much company, and her eyebrow went up. Mom, I just couldn't stand that look again. So I told her, 'We have something you don't. We have a Christmas Room.'"

Her feet shuffled. "I didn't mean to fib, but you should have seen how surprised she looked. I never saw Joan stuck before. She really didn't know what to say."

"But, dear," I said. "We do have a Christmas Room. But if it will make it more official, we'll make a sign for the door."

She brightened. "Oh, could we?"

"We'll do it today."

The sign was barely dry and hung when Joan arrived. She rarely came to our house, always preferring her house where there were lots of toys. Now she stood at our door asking to see the Christmas Room.

Barbara looked at me. "May I show her?"

"I guess so," I answered. "If everything is wrapped, that is." Barbara went to check while I explained to Joan, "The room is full of surprises, and we can't let any secrets out."

Barbara hurried back into the room. "It's okay."

Joan would probably see only a small dingy room with a cracked ceiling and a homemade sign on the door. She would not see the specialness that room held for us.

They were gone so long, I finally went and peered in. Joan was looking at our paper crèche figures we had cut out.

"We have china figures," she said. "Imported."

I started to speak, but just then Joan moved to the packages that were on the daybed. She touched them one by one, lingering over the one with the paper sled on it. Barbara had done that one from colored paper, filling the sled with miniature packages.

Joan turned to Barbara. "We don't have surprises. I always know everything."

Barbara asked, "Do you peek?"

Joan shook her head. "They ask what I want, and I get it."

Barbara said impulsively, "I'll give you a surprise."

Joan shrugged. "If you want."

Barbara nodded solemnly, before I could stop her.

During the next week, we tossed ideas about. At last, we settled on giving her one afternoon a week at our house, helping to make surprises. I wasn't sure she would think it was a present. She did come, however.

The first time, we made cookies and wrapped some for her mother. The next week, it was fancy matchboxes for her father. The week before Christmas, Barbara gave her a box to open. Joan tore at the paper, but when she had the lid off, she didn't know what it was. Barbara looked disappointed. I tried to force gaiety into my words, "It's corn—for popping."

When the corn was popped, Joan remarked, "I could never make this. It's too messy for our house."

I glanced at Barbara, but she was busy showing Joan how the corn could be dyed with food coloring.

"Later we'll string it for the Christmas tree," she explained. Joan worked at it, occasionally holding up the colorful string.

"They'll never hang this on our tree," she snorted.

"Would you like to come hang it on our tree?" I ventured.

Her sudden tears alarmed me. "Could I?" she asked. "I can never help trim ours. I might break things." Then, she pushed back her chair. "I'd better go now."

She got her coat and hat quickly. In the Christmas Room she hesitated, wondering whether to actually take home the things she'd made for her parents. At last she picked them up. We watched her leave, clutching her small surprises.

Barbara turned big eyes toward me and whispered, "I used to be jealous of her." That was long ago. It had been important at the time, but I'd thought it was long forgotten. Now once again I stood facing the Christmas Room.

I stepped inside a pleasant room, not at all like our homely old spare room. On the window seat were packages wrapped with special touches of childish imagination. The children ran to them.

"I made this!" Ronnie cried proudly.

"You're going to love mine, Grandma," Paula shouted.

There was no financial need for Barbara to do with her children what we had done—but I was glad she had. She'd been young that year of the Christmas Room, yet she must have known that a Christmas Room is a room for people, a room in the heart.

AN OLD LEATHER SCHOOL BAG

KAREN ORFITELLI

*U*nused tennis rackets and remnants of wallpaper rolls whack my head as I travel deep into the den closet. I yank them out of my way, determined to get to the other end and sort through the boxes of files from my teaching days. We are moving to a new home in a couple of weeks, and this closet is my final frontier. I stretch my arm into the far corner and drag a bulging box into the light.

I pull it open and plunge my hand inside. Instead of feeling the manila folders I anticipate, I feel the soft, pebbled leather of the book bag I had used during my fifteen years of teaching. I slide the bag out and touch the scratched corners. I smile, remembering how I had searched high and low for the perfect book bag to launch my teaching career. Finally, days before school had started, I strolled into a tiny leather goods store on Cape Cod, and there was the perfect bag displayed on the top shelf as if it were waiting for me. I tried it on for size, and when I looked at my reflection in the mirror, I was surprised by what I saw. This "perfect" bag was identical to the book bag that my father made for me when I was little—the bag I felt embarrassed about for years. Without another thought, I bought it.

Forgetting about cleaning the closet, my thoughts catapult back to the first week of fourth grade. I had trudged up Union Street from St. Joseph's School to my father's shoe repair shop in the center of Rockville, Connecticut. Before I got to his shop, however, the back-to-school window of Woolworth's drew me like a magnet. Orange, red, and yellow paper leaves randomly dotted the window as if they were falling to the ground. But what caught my attention was the red plaid book bag prominently displayed in the center of the window. The bag's shiny red plastic handle glittered brilliantly in the bright fall sun. The front of the bag featured a built-in pencil case that closed with a yellow-tabbed zipper. I pushed my face against the glass to get a better look at the two buckles, fashioned from the same shiny red plastic, that were perfectly placed on the top of the flap. *If I could just carry my books in that book bag,* I wished, *then I would be more like Janet and all the other girls in my class.* But I knew that buying the bag was out of the question. My father would never say yes.

I slid the strap of my brown book bag off my shoulder and dropped it to the sidewalk in front of me. The leather didn't shine in the sun, and the brass buckles were so dull that they didn't glimmer. There it lay, sprawled on the sidewalk, an old, ugly cow bag, a silent barrier between me and the red plaid book bag in the window. I remembered the day my father gave me the bag.

"Come into the back shop, Katrinka," he had said. "Look at what I made just for you."

My father's voice had been filled with pride when he showed me the fine piece of leather he had bought especially for this book bag. As he showed me the careful, reinforced stitching of each brass buckle, I saw only brown thread covering a dull fixture. When he pointed out the special design he sewed to strengthen the shoulder strap, I saw nothing but a strap that had no chance of breaking. And when he flipped the bag upside down to show me the brass "legs" he had put on the bottom, all I saw was one more homemade feature that made my book bag different from the rest of the girls'.

"None of the other kids will have one of these," he had said, handing me the bag and tousling my short brown pixie cut.

That, I knew, was true.

Right there in front of Woolworth's I closed my eyes. *Dear God, please help me to get a real book bag that I need. Thank you.*

No matter how I tried, I couldn't figure out a way to tell my father I didn't want the bag he had made me. Besides, the plaid bag cost $3.98. I didn't think we could afford it.

I pushed open the door of my father's shop and slid my book bag across the floor from the door to the back shop. I kissed my father hello, and he gave me a big hug. "How was school today, sweetheart?" he asked, shutting off his grinding machines so we could chat. I told him about my spelling test and my reading lab progress. He listened intently and then handed me a white pastry bag with a single apple turnover in it. I washed down my delectable treat with a glass of Tang and got to work bagging and tagging the dozens of pairs of shoes that were ready for our customers.

The next morning when I woke up for school, I knew that today of all days I couldn't bring my brown book bag to school. Janet had invited all the girls in our fourth grade class to her house for an after-school tea. Not only had I never been to an afternoon tea, but I had never been to Janet's house. She was the most popular girl in our class and had everything anyone would ever want. Janet had blond, curly hair that she got permed in a beauty salon, and she lived in a new one-family house on the outskirts of Rockville. Her dad worked for a big company in Hartford and did his work in an office. Janet also had the red plaid book bag *and* the matching pencil pouch from Woolworth's.

What seemed like the longest day of school finally ended, and all eight of us girls were ready to go to Janet's. I wasn't disappointed. Her house was even more beautiful than I ever could have imagined. Her foyer—she called it a *foy-yea*—was decorated with fresh flowers and a light fixture that dripped glass drops. The sky blue carpeting in her living room covered every inch of the floor, and matching curtains hung on the big picture window. The dining room looked as if it had blossomed for tea. The table was set with lace-trimmed place cards next to dainty china cups that were dotted with delicate pink rosebuds. Centered on the table in a matching ruffled platter was a tray of heart-shaped sandwiches that had no crusts. I felt as if I were visiting a princess.

Janet's mother helped her serve the tea from a silver teapot. We were almost ready for the cookies when the front door opened and Janet's dad walked in.

"Hi, Daddy!" Janet ran to greet him with outstretched arms. Without looking at her, he absently patted her on the top of the head. "Don't wrinkle my suit," he said, taking a step back.

"Oh, uh, sorry, Daddy," she said. "Would you like to meet my friends?"

"I don't have time," he said, opening his briefcase and pulling out a bunch of papers.

"Katherine," he said, addressing Janet's mother gruffly, "what is going on here?"

He meant us.

"Are we feeding half of Rockville?"

"Ron," she began apologetically, "I thought you said it was—excuse me, girls," she said and left the room for the kitchen.

The beautiful dining room became an echo chamber for the words Janet's parents exchanged.

"You know I like it to be quiet at home when I get here," he said. "We agreed that buying this house was important. How do you expect me to pay for it if I can't come home to peace and quiet? I want those kids out of here."

Janet's mother's next words were muffled. Then the kitchen door slammed, and heavy footsteps banged up the stairs.

Janet's mom came back into the dining room. "I'm sorry for that interruption, girls," she said without looking at any of us. "Let's finish our cookies, and then you can play in Janet's room until your parents pick you up."

We finished our cookies and tea in silence and then went to Janet's room. Flounces and ruffles decorated everything from the canopy atop her bed to the shower curtain in her private bathroom. Janet had a television, a radio, and her own record player. Never in all my life had I seen a room like this. It was perfect.

I thought of my own room with the on-sale pink paint that was just a few shades too bright to be pretty, the linoleum floor that was nicked and scratched, and the hand-me-down furniture. My eyes drank in every inch of eyelet lace that, up until a few minutes ago, I would have given anything to have. Right now it all made me feel empty and afraid.

My mind drifted back to the previous afternoon. I rubbed my cheek remembering the rough texture of my father's work apron when he hugged me hello. I remembered the flaky crust of the apple turnover he had bought just for me. Despite the mounds of shoes he had to repair, for those few moments that we talked, I felt as if I were the only person who mattered. He looked me in the eye and wanted to know about my day, my schoolwork, and my friends.

Janet's red plaid book bag lay atop her white desk. I ran my fingers over the grooves in the handle. The shiny plastic had scratches all over it. And the rivets that held the shoulder strap in place were pulling out from the weight of her schoolbooks. Up close, the bag, like Janet's life, didn't seem so perfect.

Suddenly, I longed to go home. I wanted to run upstairs and get my book bag out of the closet. I wanted to sit around our kitchen table where the bread had crusts and everyone smiled. I counted the minutes until my father picked me up.

And now, so many years later, I sit in my den clutching my book bag. My tears make uneven lines down its dust-covered back. For the first time, I understand how completely God had answered my prayer that day outside Woolworth's. I never did get the red plaid book bag, but He had given me exactly what I needed—and so much more. He gave me the gift of knowing that love doesn't come in rosebud china, silver teapots—or red plaid book bags. Sometimes it comes in small apartments with enough pasta to share, a special apple turnover for an afternoon snack, and a brown leather book bag, hand stitched with love. That day I learned that my father's love for me was as sturdy and genuine as the leather he made my bag from.

Why hadn't I ever told him?

I tuck my book bag back into the box and pick up the phone. I want to tell Pop how much I love and appreciate his love and all the things he's done for me over the years. But that was just not his way, nor mine. Instead, I would show my love for him just as he had shown it to me.

"Pop," I say as I pull my pasta maker from the cabinet, "why don't you come over for supper tonight?" My pasta never comes out as perfect as the store-bought pasta, but like my book bag, it is handmade with love. Somehow, I know he will understand.

Memory, that library of the soul from which I will draw knowledge and experience the rest of my life.

TOVE DITLEVSEN

THE BRIDAL BOUQUET

CHARLOTTE ADELSPERGER

Soap bubbles filled the air around the bride and groom, Julie and Mark, as they emerged from the church on a sunny July afternoon. The guests who blew the bubbles were lining the sidewalk with smiles and cheers as the couple hurried to a gleaming limousine parked on the curb.

The big car headed for the reception, Mark and Julie waving good-byes. Julie turned her eyes to her wedding bouquet of delicate pink and ivory roses. She thought of the printed words on the program: "The bride's bouquet is dedicated in loving memory of her mother, Joan Miller." Julie's throat tightened again. She took a breath of the roses' scent and then smiled at Mark.

"On to the party!" he called to the driver.

After a festive reception featuring a prime rib buffet and dancing, Julie spent private moments with her father, Clay, and gave him a lingering hug.

"Thanks for everything, Dad. It was more than wonderful."

Again she and her new husband slipped into the white limousine. Mark wrapped his arm around his bride's shoulder and pulled her close. Pastel balloons crowded her side of the seat.

The college-aged driver started for their destination, but the groom spoke up about turning another direction.

"Oh, yeah, you two said you wanted to make a stop—almost forgot. Just tell me where to go."

Mark gave him the location.

"It's a cemetery," Julie said softly. The car was quiet. "This is really important to me," she said. "My mom's buried there."

"I bet you don't get many requests like that," Mark said.

"No, sure don't." The chauffeur glanced at the couple through his rearview mirror. "But I understand...I lost my mother when I was thirteen."

At the cemetery, Julie clutched Mark's hand. What a tender sight—a bride in her long white gown and a groom in a black tuxedo, walking on sun-scorched grass, crossing grave after grave on a July evening. In her free hand, Julie gripped her bouquet. Her chin quivered as she neared her mother's gravesite. *I just had to come here—on this special day.*

When she and Mark reached the spot, they stood prayerfully in the dusk. Without a word, the bride bent down and gently laid the flowers on the headstone. She touched the raised letters of her mother's name—like she always did when she came. Thoughts of how her mother would have rejoiced in their wedding flooded her. Then she broke into tears and Mark, moist-eyed, held her to his chest for a long time. When they released, they looked down at Joan Miller's chosen Scripture engraved on the stone: "I know that my Redeemer lives" (Job 19:25).

"I'm ready," Julie said looking up. The new husband and wife walked hand in hand silently toward the limo—and the life before them.

Remembering

When I need your shoulder
Your embrace
Your smile,
When I need to see your face
For just a little while,
I reach inside my soul
To the precious memories it holds.

KIMBER ANNIE ENGSTROM

TEACUPS OF LOVE

NANCY JO SULLIVAN
FROM *MOMENTS OF GRACE*

When I was a little girl, every Sunday morning was like a holiday. After church, my family, all eleven of us, would gather in my grandmother's kitchen. Wrapped in the scents of warm cinnamon rolls and the sounds of small talk and percolating coffee, "Mema" would make her rounds, hugging us tightly, one by one, as if she hadn't seen us in years. Soon aunts and uncles and countless cousins would arrive. Everyone loved Mema.

One Sunday morning, when I was nine years old, Mema's kitchen got a little crowded. I slipped away from the noisy congestion of family into Mema's dining room. It was a much quieter place where warm sunlight streamed through paned picture windows, and gilded rose prints adorned the walls.

Next to a drop leaf table was a china hutch filled with polished teacups. During the hard years of the Great Depression, Mema had received each cup as a gift, a secondhand gift from a moneyless friend or relative.

"They're cups of love…priceless," Mema used to say.

That morning I found myself admiring the porcelain patterns of the keepsake cups: every petaled rose, each silver-edged heart, every etching of emerald ivy.

"Some day I'll collect teacups," I told myself as I pressed my hands against the glass doors of the hutch.

Mema peeked in on me from the kitchen. Drawing near, she saw me studying her collection.

"Which one do you like best?" she asked, smile wrinkles framing her cocoa brown eyes.

"That one!" I pointed to a sunlit cup; it was lavender, trimmed with strands of gold leaves.

Sixteen years later, on my wedding day, I opened a small package that Mema had wrapped with foil white paper. Underneath a lacy bow, she had tucked in a card. "Your favorite," it read. As I held the gift in my hand, I knew it would be the first teacup in my collection.

The early years of my marriage passed quickly. My husband and I didn't have much money, but I could always find a few dollars for the teacup hidden by the chipped punchbowls and worn Tupperware of a garage sale.

By the time my second child arrived, I had scraped the peeling paint from an old glass-doored cabinet, refinishing it with a coat of maple stain. Since I now had a "hutch" of my own, I gradually filled each shelf with secondhand teacups. I placed Mema's wedding gift cup in the middle of the collection—it would always remain my favorite.

But while I was busy adding cups to my hutch, Mema was giving hers away. She was growing older and weaker, a cancer invading her bones; nonetheless, she made sure that her keepsake cups found a home.

Like me, each of my sisters received one on her wedding day. So did the brides of my brothers and cousins. Every grandchild got a "cup of love."

A few weeks after my third child was born, Mema's health began to worsen. I visited Mema one last time while my husband watched the kids.

Before I reached the bedroom where she lay, I passed through her dining room. Stopping for a moment, I pressed my hands against the glass doors of the hutch and peered inside. All of the cups were gone; only lines of sunlight filled the shelves.

Moments later, I sat at her bedside.

"Mema," I whispered. "Your teacups…were they hard to give away?"

Mema took my hand. Though her breathing was labored, her eyes were warm and brown and bright.

"They were cups of love…and love is meant to be shared," she replied. As Mema drifted off to sleep, I closed my eyes with a clear and lovely image.

Mema's life was like a beautifully patterned teacup, brimming with a lifetime of unforgettable tenderness, given to our family as a gift.

She was like a "keepsake" passed down to us from God, ours to cherish deeply, ours to admire forever in the "hutches" of our hearts.

A few years have passed since Mema died. I miss her, but my three young daughters remind me that she is never really far away.

Recently, on a sunlit Sunday morning, I watched them study my shelved array of keepsake cups.

Together, they memorized the porcelain patterns: every petaled rose, each silver-edged heart, every etching of emerald ivy.

"Which one do you like best?" I asked Rachael, my youngest.

She pointed to a lavender cup trimmed with strands of golden leaves. "That one!"

A DESK FOR MY DAUGHTER

GARDNER MCFALL

When I was nine and about to enter fourth grade, my mother surprised me by giving me a desk. She bought it for seventy-five dollars at an outdoor auction, and I dimly recall the rap of the auctioneer's gavel, signaling that the circa-1900, fan-front, slant-top desk was mine.

It was oak, a smooth honey color, stained just dark enough to "look important," according to my mother. The leaf opened to become a solid writing surface. The cabinet held three recessed filing slots, a letter holder and, in the center, a space for items like glue and tape. Above that was a drawer, which soon enough held my crayons and collection of seaweed mounted on index cards.

The desk had two larger drawers below the bracketed shelves. At first I put stuffed animals on the shelves and later books. On the front, the keyhole's brass plate, which I loved instantly, was fancifully etched with a bird flying up toward a crescent moon and a tree tossed by the wind. And it came with a key that worked. Open or closed, the desk was a marvel. But the most marvelous feature couldn't be seen at a glance, as I discovered the day it was moved into my room.

Seated at it, I removed the small center drawer from its slip, and as I did, another drawer fell down from above—a secret compartment accessible when eased down its slanted tracks. Not even the auctioneer had mentioned this secret drawer. I thought my desk was the finest in the world.

From fourth through twelfth grades, I worked at this desk, writing my first poem, reading letters from the friends separated from me by our transient military life, and writing to my father when he was overseas. I filled out my college application on its sturdy leaf and, more than once during those years, put my head down on it and wept about some now-forgotten matter. For a child in a Navy family, pulling up stakes every two years was hard, but my desk anchored me. It became a kind of repository for all my young selves and lives. It was a constant. ·

This afternoon we are standing outside our apartment building in New York waiting for the desk to be delivered from Florida. All day she has been anticipating its arrival. I hardly know what it means to her; she hasn't ever asked for a desk, but she's as excited as if awaiting her best friend.

When the van finally appears, she leaps up and down, yelling, "Mommy, it's here!" and something inside me leaps, too. The driver, a Jacksonville antique dealer and family friend, greets us and slides open the door. I see my desk, wrapped in blankets, sandwiched between a highboy and a bedroom bureau. It looks tiny to me, but I know that to my daughter it is enormous.

With my husband's help, the driver maneuvers it up to our apartment on a dolly. After he's gone and my daughter and I are in her room, the desk in its corner, I put my arms around her and say simply, "My mother bought this for me when I was going into fourth grade, and now I want you to have it, because you're going into third."

She gives me a gripping hug and bounds off to put her treasures away—pencils in their holder, diary in one of the file slots. She stands the painted bookends made at summer camp on the top ledge. As I turn to leave her to this greatest of pleasures, she calls after me in an emphatic, rather grown-up way, "Now life's getting organized!"

But I know it's herself beginning to organize, along with her crayons, markers, sketch pads, and collection of bears soon to be installed on the bottom shelves. Should I tell her about the secret compartment, I wonder, halfway down the hall, and what I kept in it—beach glass, Beatles cards, things too small or precious to be kept anywhere else? Should I point out the key or the little bird flying up to the moon?

I decide not to. I will let her find them and make of her desk what she will. I like to think that one day in the next century, she'll give it to her own daughter and say, "Your great-grandmother bought this desk at an auction. It has many secrets and charms. See how many you can find."

Memory is the treasurer and guardian of all things.

Cicero

PRECIOUS GIFTS

ALICE GRAY
FROM *GENTLE IS A GRANDMOTHER'S LOVE*

s I look around our home, my heart always lingers longest on reminders that I am a grandmother.

Tiny wild violets and sunshiny dandelions, now dry and faded, brighten the corner of my desk. My granddaughter picked them one brisk morning many summers ago. With my finger I trace the barely visible crack in a silver-edged teacup, remembering our tea party. We dressed ourselves and the teddy bears in old-fashioned hats and gloves and held our pinkie fingers out daintily as we sipped sugar water tea. (We were *very* sophisticated.) Inside a drawer, some of the dearest treasures are safely tucked away. I unwrap white tissue paper from a round clay plaque and measure my hand against the hand print of a four-year-old. It seems like only yesterday when I held that small hand in my own.

The years pass quickly, but I am enjoying this wonderful season of being a grandmother. A newborn grandchild curls a tiny hand around Grandma's finger...and a new legacy of love begins. Once again we get to make cardboard forts in our living room. There's another chance to walk hand-in-small-hand on a starlit night and find the Milky Way. We can open a storybook we have saved for years and read, almost by heart, words from well-worn pages. We give sweet good-night kisses and say quiet bedtime prayers. We use names like "Precious" no matter how old they get, soothe bumped knees, and offer encouragement when the way seems hard. Most of all, we help young hearts understand the great love of God.

Among all the keepsakes, I cherish one most—not only because my granddaughter picked it out for me, but because she hugged me tight and whispered that the words were true. It is a small ceramic paperweight, shaped like an open book with gilded edges, delicate pink rose buds, and a pastel blue ribbon decorating the pages. An unknown author has written:

> *Grandma,*
> *Of all the beautiful gifts*
> *that come from heaven above,*
> *None could be more precious*
> *than the gift of your love.*

A grandchild is a precious gift, and so is a grandmother's love.

THE SUMMER OF THE GOLDEN EGGS

LaRayne Meyer

When I was nine, I played marbles on the wooden front stoop that led to our paint-peeling Nebraska farm house. On the patch of powdery dry buffalo grass that used to be our front lawn, I cut clothes from the Montgomery Ward catalog for my paper doll family.

When the wind from Oklahoma blew our way and its red clay haze eclipsed the sun, we finished fitful nights of sleep, punctuated by the sound of heat-parched hens dropping off their roosts.

I had an inkling problems were underfoot when my dad loaded the plow he'd bought at the end of the twenties onto our old pickup truck. The plow had been financed before half the banks went out of business and the income on our farm dropped in half. He was perplexed later that day when he stopped at the kitchen door to show Mother the machinery still on the truck. He repeated to her the dealer's words: "Take it back home. Maybe you'll be able to pay me someday. What good will it do us to take your plow? I can't figure that anybody around here could buy it anyway."

I never realized how deprived we were. I know now my mother was a master of illusion. Through it all, she sang. When she heard of the neighbor's penny auction farm sale, it was "Heaven Help Us All" and "Brother Can You Spare a Dime," as she peeled the small pile of shriveled potatoes for supper. Happy songs when the sun wasn't cooking the crops. "Amazing Grace" when the mercury boiled to the top of the thermometer. On days the sun wouldn't relent, frying the few parched stalks clinging to the cornfields, she strummed "So Long," a Dust Bowl ballad, on her guitar.

Dragging bucket after bucket of cooling water to our few fruit trees and meager garden, she crooned the spiritual, "Swing Low, Sweet Chariot." Her voice was tinged with laughter, but also carried an edge of fatigue.

The day after the grasshoppers descended, I realized life was not so simple. Mr. Tusek, our neighbor to the north, dropped by to borrow some straw, only we knew he'd never replace it.

He walked across the pasture in his bare feet, the bottoms toughened by years without shoes. He plopped down on the front stoop, pulling sandburs from his leathery arches. As he spoke, I arranged them into little bundles.

"I want to know if I can git some straw from you, Adolph," he asked my father. "I fed the last from my mattress to my horse. I've been sleeping in the yard, but the mosquitoes are about to eat me alive. I was wondering if I could git some straw from you to fill it again."

Mr. Tusek studied the ground, rolling his straw hat in his large, workworn hands, fingering the oily, green visor attached to the brim.

"Sure, Ivan," Father said. "We've got some straw up overhead in the hog barn. It's pretty dusty from the pigs. Might be full of lice, but you're welcome to it. All you need."

Mr. Tusek nodded. "The floor's getting pretty hard at home," he mumbled.

"Tell you what," Father said, settling himself on the stoop between Mr. Tusek and me. I could tell he'd been mulling something over in his mind. "I hear there's been a corn crop in Iowa and they need pickers for the harvest. What say you and me go over there and see what we find?"

Father ruffled the back of my hair. "You and Mom will be all right here without me, now, won't you?" I wondered whether he said it more to assure me or himself.

Father and Mr. Tusek made plans to leave the following week. We could handle the few chores, Mother assured Father, with a nod to me. The milk cow was dry now, along with everything else. We'd sold the calf and pigs to pay bills. Fruit and vegetables from the year before had been packed in canning jars and slowly rationed.

Father had shot all the rabbits around, scrawny things, not much meat on the bones. But with the rabbits gone, the coyotes had gotten brave. They came right onto the place, sneaking into the chicken coop, helping themselves.

So the last night before Father's trip with Mr. Tusek, Mother opened the door and let the last hen roost in the trees. Father decided, as a special treat, to take the gun and make his scanty departure supper more festive with the addition of chicken and dumplings. The hen hadn't laid eggs for months anyway, and it would lessen the guilt my father felt by providing us with a feast before he left.

He pulled the last two shells from the cupboard and went outside where the hen had flown high into the treetops, safe from predators…she thought.

We heard one quick shot and then after a ponderous silence, another shot.

"Ah," said my mother. "I've got the water boiling. We'll make quick work of picking and savoring this bird."

It was the only time I ever heard my father cry. We saw him out on the stoop, Mother and I, the gun spent, lying in the dirt.

"Stay here," she ordered.

I heard bits and pieces of the conversation, shushed and tense, through the open kitchen window.

"Now there'll be no meat…failed again…have to leave in the morning…"

"We'll be fine. We just need to have faith, that's all…"

"Nobody up there's listening…the last two shells…she's still perched up there, no use to anybody…"

When Mother and Father came into the house, their faces were tear-stained and mottled. We sat down to a supper of dumplings. Just dumplings. Dry, without eggs or chicken broth to pour over them.

Father left the next morning, gaining a little bravado with the forced smile he gave Mr. Tusek who walked up the lane. He started up the pickup and as the two headed for Iowa, I heard the strains of "So Long."

Father didn't know until he came home seven weeks later that the old hen, the one he'd used his last two shells on, that worthless, exasperating old hen, laid one egg every morning. One egg, neatly laid in the straw-lined nest of the henhouse starting the day he left with Mr. Tusek. One little life-renewing, faith-restoring egg that my mother found, gave thanks for each morning, divided in half, and shared with me. That summer, even her faith was dazzled by the golden eggs.

HANDS OF LOVE

GAIL SOSINSKY WICKMAN
FROM *GIFTS FROM OUR GRANDMOTHERS*

As a child, I never thought my grandmother's hands would stop. They knitted, crocheted, quilted, sewed. At times her hands seemed to have a life of their own. They embroidered fine stitches while my grandmother carried on lively conversations. They created patterned and beaded necklaces when she seemed half-asleep.

She created to sell; she created to give. She shunned idleness—not for fear that quiet hands would be the devil's workshop. She created because her hands demanded usefulness, because her hands desired beauty and pattern and order. To my grandmother, life and action were one.

As she aged, her hands sought simpler tasks, more suited to cataracts and arthritis. And when her making hands were finally still, I realized that these hands were my inheritance.

I see them daily as I embroider my mother's Christmas gift, sew a princess costume for my daughter, or mend the world's most precious teddy bear for my son. The project bag is ever present in my living room, bemusing my husband, who knows we can afford to buy the gifts we give.

Making is my comfort. Cloth against chaos. Immortality in pillowcase. The patterns of life shaped in embroidery floss. Creativity given substance.

When I touch my grandmother's lone-star quilt, my hands—her hands—become the hands of all women, battling decay and anonymity with a needle and thread. As each stitch connects top to bottom, fabric to fabric, so those stitches connect me, life to life, love to love.

I thank my God upon every remembrance of you.

PHILIPPIANS 1:3

Faith

STREAMS IN THE DESERT

*Like a refreshing fountain
faith bursts through the boundaries of the mind
watering the deserts of the heart.*

KIMBER ANNIE ENGSTROM

THE PRICE OF
A MIRACLE

AUTHOR UNKNOWN

Sally was only eight years old when she heard Mommy and Daddy talking about her little brother, Georgi. He was very sick, and they had done everything they could afford to save his life. Only a very expensive surgery could help him now…and that was out of the financial question. She heard Daddy say it with a whispered desperation, "Only a miracle can save him now."

Sally went to her bedroom and pulled her piggybank from its hiding place in the closet. She shook all the change out on the floor and counted it carefully. Three times. The total had to be exactly perfect. No chance here for mistakes. Tying the coins up in a cold-weather kerchief, she slipped out of the apartment and made her way to the corner drugstore.

She waited patiently for the pharmacist to give her attention…but he was too busy talking to another man to be bothered by an eight-year-old. Sally twisted her feet to make a scuffing noise. She cleared her throat. No good. Finally she took a quarter from its hiding place and banged it on the glass counter. That did it!

"And what do you want?" the pharmacist asked in an annoyed tone of voice. "I'm talking to my brother."

"Well, I want to talk to you about my brother," Sally answered back in the same annoyed tone. "He's sick…and I want to buy a miracle."

"I beg your pardon," said the pharmacist.

"My Daddy says only a miracle can save him now, so how much does a miracle cost?"

"We don't sell miracles here, little girl. I can't help you."

"Listen, I have the money to pay for it. Just tell me how much it costs."

The well-dressed man stooped down and asked, "What kind of a miracle does your brother need?"

"I don't know," Sally answered. A tear started down her cheek. "I just know he's really sick, and Mommy says he needs an operation. But my folks can't pay for it…so I have my money."

"How much do you have?" asked the well-dressed man.

"A dollar and eleven cents," Sally answered proudly. "And it's all the money I have in the world."

"Well, what a coincidence," smiled the well-dressed man. "A dollar and eleven cents…the exact price of a miracle to save a little brother."

He took her money in one hand and with the other hand he grasped her mitten and said, "Take me to where you live. I want to see your brother and meet your parents."

That well-dressed man was Dr. Carlton Armstrong, renowned surgeon specializing in solving Georgi's malady. The operation was completed…without charge, and it wasn't long until Georgi was home again and doing well. Mommy and Daddy were happily talking about the chain of events that had led them to this place.

"That surgery," Mommy whispered. "It's like a miracle. I wonder how much it would have cost?"

Sally smiled to herself. She knew exactly how much a miracle cost…one dollar and eleven cents.

Plus the faith of a little child.

THE BREATH OF GOD

Yitta Halberstam and Judith Leventhal
from *Small Miracles II*

Life's a little thing!" Robert Browning once wrote. But a little thing can mean a life. Even two lives. How well I remember. Two years ago in downtown Denver, my friend Scott Reasoner and I saw something tiny and insignificant change the world, but no one else even seemed to notice.

It was one of those beautiful Denver days. Crystal clear, no humidity, not a cloud in the sky. We decided to walk the ten blocks to an outdoor restaurant rather than take the shuttle bus that runs up and down the Sixteenth Street Mall. The restaurant, in the shape of a baseball diamond, was called The Blake Street Baseball Club. The tables were set appropriately on the grass infield. Many colorful pennants and flags hung limply overhead. As we sat outside, the sun continued to beat down on us, and it became increasingly hot. There wasn't a hint of a breeze, and heat radiated up from the tabletop. Nothing moved, except the waiters, of course. And they didn't move very fast, either.

After lunch, Scott and I started to walk back up the mall. We both noticed a mother and her young daughter walking out of a card shop toward the street. She was holding her daughter by the hand while reading a greeting card. It was immediately apparent to us that she was so engrossed in the card that she did not notice a shuttle bus moving toward her at a good clip. She and her daughter were one step away from disaster when Scott started to yell. He hadn't even gotten a word out when a breeze blew the card out of her hand and over her shoulder. She spun around and grabbed at the card, nearly knocking her daughter over. By the time she picked up the card from the ground and turned back around to cross the street, the shuttle bus had whizzed by her. She never even knew what almost happened.

To this day two things continue to perplex me about this event: Where did that one spurt of wind come from to blow the card out of that young mother's hand? There had not been a whisper of wind at lunch or during our long walk back up the mall. Second, if Scott had been able to get his words out, the young mother might have looked up at us as they continued to walk into the bus. It was the wind that made her turn back to the card—in the one direction that saved her life and her daughter's. The passing bus did not create the wind. On the contrary, the wind came from the opposite direction. I have no doubt it was a breath from God protecting them both.

But the awesomeness of this miracle is that she never knew. As we continued back to work, I wondered how often God acts in our lives without our being aware. The difference between life and death can very well be a little thing.

ANIMAL CRACKERS

Jennifer Tovell

The asphalt walkway was a beautiful thing to roller skate on, with its little hills and valleys that you could almost effortlessly glide on, ever so smoothly.

I frequented the housing complex with my metal skates clipped on over the toes of my shoes and the leather strap buckled around my ankles. What a beautiful feeling, to glide along in the sun, feeling the summer breeze in my hair. It made me feel like I hadn't a care in the world.

One afternoon I took my time there enjoying the warm afternoon with no reason to hurry home for supper. I knew there would be no "real" dinner waiting. These last few days were the leanest my family had ever known.

My mother was great at making something-out-of-practically-nothing taste good, but even the practically-nothings seemed to be just about gone.

But as a kid, you don't worry too much about things like that. My sister and I would make grape jelly sandwiches (if there was any bread and jelly, and peanut butter was usually just a wish), but there was always a book to read to take my mind off my growling tummy. I especially liked to read Dr. Seuss. But this day, I knew, would be a long one, with lots of tummy-growling, lots of reading.

As the sun began to settle, resting after blazing long in the summer sky, I turned to go home. There may not have been food there, but it was my home and my family was there, and a book.

I skated back on the smooth, winding asphalt walkway making my way home. As the light in the sky grew dimmer, I could almost feel the night entering my soul.

I crossed the street and headed for our doorway. We lived in a small, second floor apartment next to Sam's Fish Market. My mom used to go in there and ask if she could buy food "on credit," with a promise to pay him as soon as she got some money. Sam was usually kind enough to allow it. Seeing she had a large family, how could he turn her away? But she couldn't go in there these days. No, the bill was getting just a little too high and my mother was a proud woman.

I turned toward our stoop and the big glass door that loomed just past it when I noticed there was something there. *Someone must have left something here,* I thought. *I wonder if they're coming back?*

Then, as though a light switch was thrown on in my head, it registered just what it was. Two large, *very* large, brown grocery bags, just brimming with food!

There was long, crusty bread hanging over the top of one of them, and when I peeked inside I could see spaghetti and rice and cans of vegetables and sauce and—*cookies!* Animal crackers they were, to be precise. My favorite!

I think my heart just leaped to the sky with happiness as I realized that maybe, just maybe, this food was left for us. But who would have left it here? It didn't matter. Mom would be so happy!

I tore off my skates and grabbed one of the bags and ran upstairs just as fast as I could, making sure not to let anything spill out.

"Mom, Mom!" I cried, as I ran huffing and puffing up the stairs. I was so out of breath from the excitement that I could barely answer her question of where the food came from as I practically crash-landed the bag on the kitchen table.

"Mom, Mom!" I cried. "You're not going to believe this, but there's *another bag!* There's *another bag!* I don't know who forgot them on our step, but can we keep them?"

My mother was silent but so overjoyed that tears came to her eyes. She didn't jump up and shout like I did, and I don't think she even got out of breath when she went down the stairs to get the other bag.

She just closed her eyes and said, "Thank You for hearing my prayer."

At that moment, I joyfully figured we were keeping the food as she seemed to know who left it for us.

Prayer is not primarily going to God for what we want.
It's God drawing us close to carry out what He wants.

CHARLOTTE ADELSPERGER

MY FIRST CHRISTMAS
IN HEAVEN

AUTHOR UNKNOWN

This poem is alleged to have been written by a teen boy who died of a brain tumor he had battled for four years. He gave this to his mom before he died.

I see the countless Christmas trees
Around the world below,
With tiny lights, like heaven's stars,
Reflecting on the snow.
The sight is so spectacular,
Please wipe away the tear,
For I am spending Christmas with
Jesus Christ this year.
I hear the many Christmas songs
That people hold so dear,
But the sounds of music can't compare
With the Christmas choir up here.
I have no words to tell you
The joy their voices bring,
For it is beyond description

To hear the angels sing.
I know how much you miss me,
I see the pain inside your heart.
But I am not so far away,
We really aren't apart.
So be happy for me, dear ones,
You know I hold you dear.
And be glad I'm spending Christmas
With Jesus Christ this year.
I sent you each a special gift
From my heavenly home above.
I sent you each a memory
Of my undying love.
After all, love is a gift more precious
Than pure gold.
It was always most important
In the stories Jesus told.
Please love and keep each other,
As my Father said to do.
For I can't count the blessing or love
He has for each of you.
So have a Merry Christmas and
Wipe away that tear.
Remember, I am spending Christmas with
Jesus Christ this year.

MOM'S OLD BIBLE

JERRY B. JENKINS
FROM *THE STORY JAR*

Late one night when I was a teenager, I took a good look at my mother's old Bible. The crumbling cover and dog-eared pages brought back memories of bedtime prayers. I thought of Mom when she was Mommy.

An inscription from Dad dates the Bible from before my birth. Mom's maiden name was barely readable on the cover. Two references were penned onto the dirty first page. One—John 3:5—is unmistakably written by my oldest brother, Jim. The backward scrawl reminded me of those years when the old Bible was passed around, carried to church, and claimed as "mine" by three different boys. Mom didn't often get to carry the Bible herself while we were growing up, but we frequently found her reading it at home when we came in from paper routes or baseball games.

The other reference on that first page was Psalm 37:4 in Mom's handwriting. I turned to the chapter and saw that Mom had underscored the verbs in the first five verses. *"Fret not* thyself because of evildoers.... *Trust* in the LORD, and do good.... *Delight* thyself also in the LORD.... *Commit* thy way unto the LORD; *trust* also in him; and he shall bring it to pass."

But apparently her favorite part was *"Delight* thyself also in the LORD; and He shall give thee the desires of thine heart."

On the next page, is the inscription from Dad: "To Bonnie, in loving remembrance of October 21, 1942. Your devoted Red. Matthew 19:6."

He'd been nearly nineteen, she sixteen, when they were engaged. World War II and his thirty-two months in the Pacific delayed their marriage until December 1945.

I turned the next page. "Hello, everybody." Jim's writing again, probably kindling someone's indignation, but the words were never scratched out, and they remain as a child's warm welcome for anyone who cares to open Mom's old Bible.

On the next page Jim wrote "The Way of Salvation" with a verse for each of five steps. Despite the inconsistent strokes of the preteen writer, the guidelines are still there for men of all ages who want, as Jim pointed out in step three, a "way of escape."

Scanning the page, I noted several of Mom's markings, countless underlinings of promises and passages that look to heaven. The penciled markings had faded, and the inked jottings had bled through to other pages. But the evidence remained of well-listened-to sermons and cherished hours alone in the Word.

In the back, after the concordance, the guides, and the maps, Mom listed several references to crown of joy, righteousness, life, and glory. Looking up 1 Thessalonians 2:19 showed me again that Mom loved to rejoice in the thought of Christ's return.

On the last page of Mom's Bible, she again wrote "Psalm 37:4." That last inscription is framed by the doodling of youthful hands. One of the desires of Mom's heart was that her little boys would grow up and do something more profitable with those once-small hands. Mom's first desire, she told us, was that her four boys would make decisions to trust Christ. We have all done that.

Mom still delights herself in the Lord, which is a continual encouragement for me to do something constructive with the hands that scribbled in her Bible so many years ago.

Mom's old Bible reminds me of her hands. Hands that held, spanked, mended, and wiped tears; hands that produced a magic knot in the shoelaces on my three-year-old feet.

Mom's hands turned the pages of her old Bible for me until I learned to read it myself.

The Twenty-Third Psalm for Women

✦

The Lord is my peace. I shall not live in anxiety. He puts me under His wings of comfort and calms my spirit within me. He takes all my anxieties on Himself and helps me to focus on Him. Yes, though I walk through a time of grave uncertainties and fierce anxieties, I will not fret—for You are my peace. Your Word and Your presence calm me now. You hold my uncertainties in the palm of Your hand. You smooth my wrinkled brow. Surely serenity and trust in You shall fill me all the days of my life. And I shall keep my mind stayed on You forever.

JUDY BOOTH
FROM *CALM MY ANXIOUS HEART*

MAY I HAVE THIS DANCE?

NANCY JO SULLIVAN
FROM *MOMENTS OF GRACE*

ordered a bag of popcorn at the snack bar while my girls scurried through the department store searching for Christmas gifts. I yawned as the clerk handed me my snack; I could barely keep my eyes open.

We had just moved into a new home. In between unpacking boxes, I had baked cookies and wrapped presents and written cards of greeting.

So far the holidays had left me feeling depleted of energy. I hadn't even had time for prayer or quiet reflection. I wanted to feel close to God, especially in this season, but I was just too tired.

As I settled into a booth, I noticed an old, kind-faced man standing near the store entryway—he was ringing a Salvation Army bell. Though his face was wrinkled, his eyes bore the energetic twinkle of youth.

Wearing bib overalls and an ear-muffed hat, the man's skin was much darker than the lighter-faced customers who crowded the suburban store.

I watched as he danced around his red coin kettle, bobbing and turning to the rhythm of his own footsteps. Ringing his bell in carefully timed beats, he waved and smiled to those who passed him by.

"Joy to the world…whoa…the Lord…mmm…the Lord has come."

Soon a woman made her way past the singing man. She was wearing a Christmas tree sweater trimmed with ribbons and baubles. She dodged her way past the man; her brow was furrowed and she carried several shopping bags.

"No joy for the Lord?" the Salvation Army worker called out to her.

The woman sighed and rolled her eyes. She hurried to her car.

I watched as people hustled past the man; most of them ignored his presence. Everyone seemed to be preoccupied with balancing the bags and boxes that contained their purchases.

A businessman with a cell phone walked past the dancing bell ringer.

"Let every heart…mmm…prepare Him room…" the dark-skinned man sang.

The businessman kept walking as the beeping noise from the cash registers forced him to shout his conversation into the phone. He reminded me of all the obligations I had for the season. I was trying to find a way to converse with God, but so far I hadn't gotten a good connection.

As countless shoppers made a point to walk a wide perimeter around the coin collector, an older woman drew near.

Though her back was hunched and her gait was slow, she smiled as she clicked open a purse decorated with beads. She dropped four quarters into the slotted red pail.

The man took off his ear-muffed hat and bowed to her.

"May I have this dance?" he asked.

The woman began to giggle and blush. As she straightened up, it almost seemed as if her wrinkles were beginning to fade.

The two of them began to shuffle around the store entryway, the man in overalls gently guiding the frail woman in graceful glides and turns.

"Joy to the world…the Savior reigns…" their voices rang out in happy refrain.

As I watched, I found myself wanting to join their department store waltz. Theirs was a dance of Christmas joy, a dance unencumbered by stress or preoccupations, a dance of praise, a dance that proclaimed anew the tender message of old: "Joy to the world…the Lord has come!"

Later that night, as my family slept upstairs, I curled up on the couch in our family room.

Turning on my favorite holiday CD, I drank a cup of tea in front of our brightly lit tree. Soon a guitar version of "Joy to the World" filled the room.

I imagined God bowing before me. I could almost hear Him say: "May I have this dance?"

I bless the holy name of God with all my heart.
Yes, I will bless the Lord and not forget
the glorious things he does for me.

PSALM 103:1–2
THE LIVING BIBLE

BLOSSOMS OF KINDNESS

BETTY KEHL
FROM *RIPPLES OF JOY*

I remember last spring watching the first shoots of grass lifting their heads and testing the air. The grass didn't seem to grow fast enough after the long Wisconsin winter.

To nurture my longing for spring, I visited the local garden center, all the time dreaming about summer: birds chirping, warm breezes, cats pouncing on imaginary bugs before reclining beside the flower bed as I worked.

Finally it seemed safe enough to purchase the plants without putting them through a late frost. Pansies were my choice; their hooded faces seemed always smiling as they danced in God's creation. Having a very small garden, I had to choose every plant painstakingly. Sunny yellow and purple, a calm peach, majestic white and purple, velvet purple with specks of yellow.

As I was paying for the plants, the cashier commented on the stately beauty of a gigantic white-and-purple pansy. It did seem to stand out over all of the rest, and I nodded with pride, mentally planting it in the center of my garden with all of the other flowers around it, paying homage.

After I returned home, just as I was about to begin tenderly transplanting the pansies, my eight-year-old neighbor, Kim, came over to

292

investigate. Her eyes lit up when she saw the flowers. Kim's family doesn't plant a garden, so the year before I had given her a pansy to plant next to her house. This seemed like a good tradition to keep up, so I asked her if she was ready to pick a pansy. She smiled, knelt down, and longingly touched the petals of several plants.

Somehow I recognized myself in this eight-year-old. I held my breath, though, as she constantly came back to my prized white-and-purple pansy. The other flowers were so colorful—surely the white pansy would be safe! But, no, Kim's blue eyes were sparkling as she picked up the "white king" and sprinted to her house with her new prize.

As I adjusted my mental picture of my garden—without the giant pansy at its center—I felt a sense of loss. A flower is such a small thing, but that pansy was a difficult one to give up. I knew it was right, however, to give, and I remembered that God wants us to give of our "firstfruits." I decided that rather than feel bad, I would rejoice that I could give such a remarkable flower to a little friend.

And all summer God blessed me for my hesitant gift. Kim and her dad planted the pansy by the corner of their house. There it prospered, and I saw it every time I drove into my driveway. I smiled every time I passed it.

But God wasn't finished blessing me yet. I had planted some bushes the summer before, highlighting them with a one-time planting of pansies. I had planted no seeds or seedlings around them this year, yet pansy after pansy, with no help from me, pushed through the earth and blossomed. Every time I admired God's garden, I thought of Ecclesiastes 11:1: "Give generously, for your gifts will return to you later" (TLB).

And still God was not finished with His blessings. Recently, after several frosts, I stepped outside into an unusually warm day for a Wisconsin November. Walking around the grounds, I noticed empty birds' nests in bare trees and leaves spinning over the ground. When I came to my garden, everything was brown and frozen and dead...except for one giant, perfectly formed pansy growing in the middle of my garden! I knelt to examine it. The purple-and-white petals were so soft to the touch....

SNOWFLAKES FROM HEAVEN

LINDA HOHONSHELT

ost of us are familiar with the saying that "God works in mysterious ways." Whenever I hear that phrase, it takes me back to a beautiful spring day in late April when I was twelve years old.

My closest friend, Cheryl, had come home with me after school to spend the night and would ride the bus to school with me the next day. It was a very warm day, and we stayed outside until dinnertime.

Often, Cheryl had talked to me about God, and I had gone to church with her a couple of times. That night just before going to bed, she told me that God could do anything. So I threw out a challenge.

"Can He make it snow so we won't have to go to school tomorrow?" I asked curiously. We lived in the country at the top of a long hill, and when there was a heavy snow, the school bus couldn't make it to our house.

"If He wants to, He can," she replied.

"Then let's pray and ask Him to make it snow!" I was excited. If God could do anything—even make it snow in late April—I was all for asking Him to do it. The school bus wouldn't be able to get up the hill, and we could spend the *whole* day together. So we prayed.

The next morning, my mother came to wake us up and told us that we wouldn't be going to school. It had snowed! Cheryl and I flew out of bed and ran downstairs. I will never forget opening the front door. We stood in the doorway with our mouths open. Everything was covered in snow. And not just a little snow—a lot of snow—so much snow that the school bus couldn't make it up the hill. God had answered our prayer!

Cheryl and I played in the snow off and on all day until her parents came to pick her up that afternoon. The first snowfall of each year since then brings to mind the extraordinary events of that day. God affected the lives of thousands of people with an abundant snowfall to reveal His amazing love for a twelve-year-old girl. It proved to me that He *does* exist and that He *can* do anything—a truth that has carried me throughout my life.

Road Map

Many times I long for a road map
With one highway
Clearly marked in red ink...
Showing my journey
From first to last
From beginning to end,
With all the bypasses
And detours
And dead ends
Circled.
Then I realize
How dull the way would seem
To know every turn up ahead.
God had a better idea.
He chose to show me the way
A day at a time...
Promising to make a roadway in the wilderness.
Who needs a map
When He says,
"Follow Me!"

BARBARA DARLAND

THE CHRISTMAS I REMEMBER MOST

ROBIN JONES GUNN

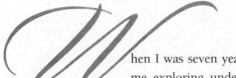hen I was seven years old, my grandma caught me exploring under her bed two days before Christmas. I found dozens of presents and I pleaded with her:

"Please, Grandma, can't I open just one? Please?"

"Oh, no, no!" she cautioned me. "Not until after the Christmas Eve candlelight service."

I shuffled into the living room and fiddled with the manger scene on the coffee table. Mary, Joseph, the shepherds, and baby Jesus in the manger. I knew the whole story. But it was the Christmas tree in the corner that intrigued me the most. All those wonderful ornaments and the presents that would soon be opened!

Christmas Eve day was the longest I'd ever experienced. Finally, Mom dressed me in my red velvet dress and our whole family drove to church.

I endured the service by snuggling up against the fur collar on Grandma's red coat. All I could think about were those presents which had moved from under the bed to under the tree. When we stood to sing, Grandma sang the high notes in a trilly, birdlike way that I thought was beautiful.

Everything was beautiful about Grandma that night. Beautiful and soft. Especially her hands. She held mine as we prayed, and she let me twist her gold wedding band around and around her finger. We sang again and her voice rose high like a flute on "Let Earth Receive Her King!" I felt like Grandma was celebrating something very special and I wanted to be in on it, too.

The pastor lit a candle from the advent wreath on the altar, and then all the lights went down. Grandma reached beside her on the pew and handed one to me. I held it silently, watching with fascination as the light from the candle passed from one person to the next, diffusing the darkness with its glow.

Grandpa lit Grandma's candle, then she turned to light mine. I looked up into her soft face in the candlelight. She smiled and something inside my seven-year-old heart melted. I don't know if it was her joy or the softness or the beauty of that moment. But inside I glowed, just like the candle.

When we got home we anchored our still-burning candles onto the hearth. Somebody snapped on the stereo and plugged in the tree lights. Then everyone laughed at my brother's antics as he passed out the gifts from under the tree.

Funny thing was, I didn't open my gifts. Not at first. I kept staring at my stubby candle, watching its captivating flame glimmer and dance. I wished we were back at church. I wanted to feel my grandma's soft hands, watch her glowing face, and hear the way her voice warbled when she sang.

Until that night, I'd only known Jesus as that little baby in the manger. Grandma showed me a different Jesus. Jesus, the King. Jesus, the light of the world. Jesus, the One for whom the angels sang.

THE GREATEST QUESTION

ANNE GRAHAM LOTZ

y father was seated at a welcoming dinner in his honor attended by the civic, business, religious, and political leaders of the eastern nation that had invited him to hold open evangelistic meetings. The man next to him was the archbishop of the dominant religion in that country. During the course of the dinner conversation, my father asked the archbishop when he had become a Christian. The man's eyes glistened with emotion as he put down his fork and proceeded to tell my father his story.

He had already been installed as the archbishop in his country when he was invited to Chicago to give a lecture in a prominent theological school. He accepted the invitation and found himself in the heart of the Windy City.

One afternoon, in his effort to do some sightseeing, he boarded a city bus. No sooner had he taken his seat when a big black finger tapped him on the shoulder. He turned to look into the full, round, ebony face of an obviously poor woman seated behind him. In a wonderfully rich voice, she asked, "Mister, has you ever been born again?" He frowned, thinking for sure he had misunderstood her question since English was his second language. With polite reserve he asked, "Excuse me?"

The deep, rolling voice repeated, "I says, has you been born again?" The archbishop stiffened his back, straightened his shoulders, and replied with the greatest dignity, "My dear madam, I am the archbishop of the church in my country. I am here to give a lecture at the theological seminary."

As the bus rolled to a stop, the woman rose to get off. She looked at the proud, religious man dressed in his flowing robes bearing the bejeweled insignia of his office and persisted bluntly, "Mister, that ain't what I asked you. I asked you, 'Has you been born again?'" Then she turned and walked off the bus and out of his life.

But, the archbishop said, her words rang in his ears and burned in his soul. He went back to his hotel room, located a Gideon Bible in a dresser drawer, opened it to the Gospel of John, and read the familiar story of Nicodemus. With increasing clarity and conviction, he knew that even with all of his religious training and devotion and service and recognition, he had never been born again. So he slipped down on his knees, and that night, in a Chicago hotel room thousands of miles from his home, God answered his heart's cry, and just gave him Jesus.

So let us come boldly to the very throne of God
and stay there to receive his mercy and to find grace
to help us in our times of need.

HEBREWS 4:16
THE LIVING BIBLE

TOTALLY AWESOME

CHARLES R. SWINDOLL

ho is Jesus Christ? The God-man—the most unique Person who ever lived. The awesome Son of God!

Some time ago a lady wrote me a true story of an event that happened in a Christian school:

A kindergarten teacher was determining how much religious training her new students had. While talking with one little boy, to whom the story of Jesus was obviously brand new, she began relating His death on the cross. When asked what a cross was, she picked up some sticks, and fashioning a crude one, she explained that Jesus was actually nailed to that cross, and then He died. The little boy with eyes downcast quietly acknowledged, "Oh, that's too bad." In the very next breath, however, she related that He arose again and that He came back to life. And his little eyes got big as saucers. He lit up and exclaimed, "Totally awesome!"

You don't know the full identity of Jesus if your response is "Oh, that's too bad." You know His identity only if your description is "TOTALLY AWESOME!"

Because
I Care

BECAUSE I CARE

Please take a moment to read the verses written on the next page. Although there are hundreds of verses in the Bible that tell us about God's love and His gift of salvation, I chose these from the book of Romans in the New Testament.

I care about what happens to you now, but I care even more about where you will spend eternity. If you have never asked Jesus Christ to be your Savior, please consider inviting Him into your life now.

Many years ago I prayed a simple prayer that went something like this....

> *Dear Jesus,*
>
> *I believe You are the Son of God and that You gave Your life as a payment for the sins of mankind. I believe You rose from the dead and You are alive today in heaven preparing a place for those who trust in You.*
>
> *I have not lived my life in a way that honors You. Please forgive me for my sins and come into my life as Savior and Lord. Help me grow in knowledge and obedience to You.*
>
> *Thank You for forgiving me. Thank You for coming into my life. Thank You for giving me eternal life. Amen.*

If you have sincerely asked Jesus Christ to come into your life, He will never leave you or forsake you. Nothing—absolutely nothing—will be able to separate you from His love.

God bless you, dear one. I'll look forward to meeting you one day in heaven.

—*Alice Gray*

For all have sinned and fall short of the glory of God.
ROMANS 3:23

For the wages of sin is death, but the gift of God
is eternal life in Christ Jesus our Lord.
ROMANS 6:23

But God demonstrates his own love toward us in this:
While we were still sinners, Christ died for us.
ROMANS 5:8

If you confess with your mouth, "Jesus is Lord," and believe
in your heart that God raised him from the dead, you will be saved.
For it is with your heart that you believe and are justified,
and it is with your mouth that you confess and are saved.
ROMANS 10:9–10

Everyone who calls on the name of the Lord will be saved.
ROMANS 10:13

I am convinced that neither death nor life,
neither angels nor demons,
neither the present nor the future,
nor any powers, neither height nor depth
nor anything else in all creation,
will be able to separate us from the love of God
that is in Christ Jesus our Lord.
ROMANS 8:38–39

Gentle Is a Grandmother's Love

stories compiled by Alice Gray,
illustrated by Paula Vaughan

Enjoy the precious influences of a grandmother's love in these touching stories compiled by Alice Gray. Filled with poignant, heartwarming moments and enhanced by the lovely artwork of Paula Vaughan, it will be a treasure you'll return to again and again.

ISBN 1-58860-048-3

Enjoy Reading with Alice Gray from Morning Coffee to Your Afternoon Cup of Tea!

stories compiled by Alice Gray,
illustrated by Susan Mink Colclough

Quiet Reflections Journal

Capture your heart's deepest desires and your unspoken dreams in the pages of this exquisite companion journal, sumptuously illustrated by Susan Mink Colclough. Lightly ruled and graced with inspirational quotes and Scripture…a lovely treasure in tandem with *Quiet Moments and a Cup of Tea* and *Morning Coffee and Time Alone*.

Quiet Moments and a Cup of Tea

Alice Gray takes you on a quiet journey of faith, hope, and love through stories lavishly illustrated by Susan Mink Colclough. This book will be as cherished as the moments of serenity it offers.

Morning Coffee and Time Alone

Celebrate the morning and anticipate the blessings of each new day as you curl up with Alice Gray's treasure-trove of inspiring stories, Scriptures, and prose. Bringing bright promise of captured moments alone, this book is gracefully illustrated by the hand of Susan Mink Colclough.

ISBN 1-58860-009-2

ISBN 1-58860-008-4

ISBN 1-58860-007-6

Friends Are Flowers in the Garden of Life

stories compiled by Alice Gray,
illustrated by Katia Andreeva

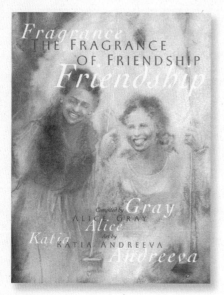

The Fragrance of Friendship

Katia Andreeva captures the lush beauty of fragrant gardens and the sweetness of the beloved bonds of friendship in this charming collection of inspirational quotes and stories. Compiled by Alice Gray, it encompasses the comfort of lifelong friendships and the joy of those found for the first time…a perfect means to express love to dear ones in your life.

ISBN 1-58860-005-X

A Pleasant Place

Alice Gray's compilation of heartwarming stories of goodness and cheer inspire you to spread some sunshine, like ripples in a pond…and be encouraged in the process. Elegantly illustrated in vivid watercolors by the gifted hand of Katia Andreeva.

ISBN 1-58860-006-8

The Stories for the Heart Series

compiled by Alice Gray

**More than
5 million
in print!**

www.storiesfortheheart.com

The Stories for the Heart Series

compiled by Alice Gray

www.storiesfortheheart.com

ACKNOWLEDGMENTS

More than a thousand books, magazines, and other sources were researched for this collection as well as a review of hundreds of stories sent by friends and readers of the *Stories for the Heart* collection. A diligent search has been made to trace original ownership, and when necessary, permission to reprint has been obtained. If we have overlooked giving proper credit to anyone, please accept my apologies. If you will contact Multnomah Publishers, Inc., Post Office Box 1720, Sisters, Oregon 97759, corrections will be made prior to additional printings. Please provide detailed information.

Notes and acknowledgments are listed by story title in the order they appear in each section of the book. For permission to reprint any of the stories, please request permission from the original source listed below. Grateful acknowledgment is made to authors, publishers, and agents who granted permission for reprinting these stories.

COMPASSION

"Don't Let It End This Way" by Sue Monk Kidd. Reprinted with permission from *Guideposts* magazine (June 1979). © 1979 by Guideposts, Carmel, NY 10512.

"May Baskets" by Faith Andrews Bedford. © 2000. Used by permission of the author. Faith Andrews Bedford writes for numerous magazines, especially *Country Living*, where her column, "Kids in the Country," appears regularly. She is the author of *Frank W. Benson: American Impressionist* and *The Sporting Art of Frank W. Benson*.

"Mrs. Amatuli" by Nanci Stroupe. © 2000. Used by permission of the author.

"Ivy's Cookies" by Candy Abbott. © 1998. True story reprinted from *Chicken Soup for the Prisoner's Soul* by permission of Candy Abbott.

"Keep Me Faithful" by Ruth Harms Calkin. From *Tell Me Again, Lord, I Forget* by Ruth Harms Calkin, Pamona, California. © 1974. Used by permission of the author. All rights reserved.

"On a Stretch of California Freeway" by Carolyn Lightfoot. Used by permission of the author. Carolyn Lightfoot lives in a lakeside community in northern Idaho and loves writing about the tenderness of God's heart and the myriad ways He moves into and through our lives with beautiful intention. E-mail her at scribbler8@msn.com.

"More than a Hero" by Jan Nations. Used by permission of the author. Jan is executive producer for a worldwide radio broadcast and has had numerous short stories published in books and magazines. She has three married children (including

TREASURED MOMENTS

"Just for Today" by Sally Meyer. © 1999. Used by permission of the author. This poem was written for my son Dhylan who has autism.

"A Dance Lesson in the Kitchen" by Marcia Lee Laycock. © 2000. Used by permission of the author. Marcia is a pastor's wife and mother of three girls. She is the author of a weekly column, "The Spur" (Hebrews 10:24), showcased on her Web site: www.vinemarc.ab.ca.

MOTHERHOOD

"Snowballs and Lilacs" by Lisa Marie Finley. Used by permission of the author.

"It Will Change Your Life" by Dale Hanson Bourke. From *Everyday Miracles: Holy Moments in a Mother's Day.* © 1989. Used by permission of Broadman & Holman.

"Nightlight" by Sue Monk Kidd. From page 149 of *When the Heart Waits* by Sue Monk Kidd. © 1990 by Sue Monk Kidd. Reprinted by permission of HarperCollins Publishers, Inc.

"Bedtime Blessings" by Nancy Jo Sullivan. © 2001. Used by permission of the author.

"My Plastic Pearls" by Judy Gordon. © 2001. Used by permission of the author.

"Heaven's Very Special Child" by Edna Massimilla. © 1956, revised 1999. Used by permission of the author and This Is Our Life Publications, Ministry for the Disabled, 2815 Byberry Road, Suite 118, Hatboro, PA 19040.

"Danger: My Mother" by Anne Goodrich. © 2001. Used by permission of the author.

"School Days" by Nancy B. Gibbs. © 1998. Used by permission of the author. Nancy B. Gibbs is a pastor's wife and the mother of three grown children. She is a weekly religion columnist and a freelance writer. She has been published by Honor Books and Guideposts Books and also in several magazines and devotional guides. She may be contacted at Daiseydood@aol.com or P.O. Box 53, Cordele, GA 31010.

"My Mother Played the Piano" by John Smith and LeAnn Weiss. From *Hugs for Mom.* © 1997. Used by permission of Howard Publishing.

"A Breath of Time" by Carla Muir. © 2000. Used by permission of the author.

"Too Many Ripples" by Cheryl Kirking. Reprinted from *Ripples of Joy.* © 2000 by Cheryl Kirking. Used by permission of WaterBrook Press, Colorado Springs, CO. All rights reserved.

"How Does She Do That?" by John Trent, Ph.D., with Erin M. Healy. Reprinted from *My Mother's Hands.* © 2000. Used by permission of WaterBrook Press, Colorado Springs, CO. All rights reserved.

FRIENDSHIP

INSPIRATION

"Two Scoops of Ice Cream" by Cynthia Hamond, S.F.O. © 2000. Used by permission of the author. Cynthia's stories have been published in magazines, both the Chicken Soup for the Soul and Stories for the Heart series, and made into a TV movie. Contact: P.O. Box 488, Monticello, MN 55362 or Candbh@aol.com.

"With Songs of Rejoicing" by Joan Wester Anderson. From *Angels We Have Heard on High* by Joan Wester Anderson. © 1997 by Joan Wester Anderson. Used by permission of Ballantine Books, a division of Random House, Inc.

"God's Promise" by Judy Gordon. © 2001. Used by permission of the author.

"Then There Was Hope" by Edd L. Brown from the June/July issue of *Lifewise* published by Focus on the Family. © 2000. Used by permission of the author.

"Best Present of All" by Bonnie Compton Hanson. From *Heart Stirring Stories of Love* by Linda Evans Shepherd. © 2000. Used by permission of Broadman & Holman, Nashville, TN 37234.

"Love Made Visible" by Bob Perks. Used by permission of the author. Bob Perks is a professional speaker/author. Visit www.BobPerks.com. E-mail Bob@BobPerks.com.

"The Perfect Dogwood" by Corrina Hyde. © 2000. Used by permission of the author.

"A Day Hemmed in Love" by Nancy Jo Sullivan. From *Moments of Grace* by Nancy Jo Sullivan. © 2000. Used by permission of Multnomah Publishers, Inc.

"Heartsong" by Jennifer Oliver. © 2000. Used by permission of the author. Hailing from Killeen, Texas, Jennifer Oliver is wife to awesome househubby, Stephen, mother to four beautiful blessings, and works full time for the government on the side. She cites Stephen as her wellspring of inspiration.

"Auntie" by Betty Johnson. © 2001. Used by permission of the author.

TRUE LOVE

"An Old-Fashioned Love Story" by Sharon Sheppard. © 1984. Used by permission of the author.

"Berry Mauve or Muted Wine?" by T. Suzanne Eller. © 2000. Used by permission of the author. Suzanne Eller is a freelance writer and inspirational speaker from Oklahoma. She can be reached at eller@intellex.com or at www.intellex.com/~eller/tseller.html.

"Anniversary Morning" by Paul Kortepeter. © Susan Wheeler, from Holly Pond Hill ® Licensed by InterArt Licensing. Used by permission.

"Ben and Virginia" by Gwyn Williams. © 1997. Used by permission of the author.

"Love in a Locket" by Geery Howe. © 1998. Used by permission of the author. Geery Howe, M.A., is a consultant, international speaker, and trainer in leadership, management, and strategic change/development. Author of *Listen to the Heart: The Transformational Pathway to Health and Wellness.* Check out his Web site at: http://members.aol.com/geeryhowe/.

"With This Ring" by Ruth Bell Graham. From *Ruth Bell Graham's Collected Poems.* © 1995. Used by permission of Baker Book House.

"Mom's Last Laugh" by Robin Lee Shope. © 1999. Used by permission of the author.

"Grace's Amazing Valentine" by Shawn Alyne Strannigan. © 2001. Used by permission of the author.

"No Scorecard" by Marguerite Murer, a professional speaker, educator, and the executive assistant to the president of the Texas Rangers Baseball Club. Combining her educational background with her unique baseball experiences, Marguerite inspires and energizes her audiences to step up to the plate and hit a home run. Marguerite can be reached at 501 Knox Place, Joliet, IL 60435, phone: 815-722-0321 or e-mail: mmurer@texasrangers.com. Used by permission of the author.

"The Treasured Ring" by Rochelle M. Pennington, newspaper columnist; contributing author to *Stories for the Heart, Chicken Soup for the Soul,* and *Life's Little Instruction Book;* and coauthor of *Highlighted in Yellow.* You may reach her at N3535 Corpus Christi Circle, Campbellsport, WI 53010, (920) 533-5880. Used by permission of the author.

"Do You Want Me?" by Park York. From the June 1989 issue of the *Christian Herald.* Used by permission of the Christian Herald Associates.

POTPOURRI

"Fragrant Medley" by Kimber Annie Engstrom. © 2001. Used by permission of the author.

"My Most Unforgettable Fare" by Kent Nerburn. Abridged from pages 57–63 from *Make Me an Instrument of Your Peace* by Kent Nerburn. © 1999 by Kent Nerburn. Reprinted by permission of HarperCollins Publishers, Inc.

"Thank You, Fozzy" by Rusty Fischer. © 2000. Used by permission of the author. Rusty Fischer is the author of *The 25 Stories of Christmas* available from xlibris.com.

"The Peacekeeper" by Gloria Cassity Stargel. © 2001. Used by permission of the author. Gloria Cassity Stargel is an assignment writer for *Guideposts* magazine and the author of *The Healing, One Family's Victorious Struggle with Cancer.* www.brightmorning.com or 1-800-888-9529.

"Yuk It Up" by Patsy Clairmont. From *Normal Is Just a Setting on Your Dryer* by Patsy Clairmont, a Focus on the Family book published by Tyndale House. Copyright © 1993 by Patsy Clairmont. All rights reserved. International copyright secured. Used by permission.

"For His Eyes Only" by Kathleen Ruckman. © 2001. Used by permission of the author. Kathleen Ruckman, mother of four, wife of a physician, freelance writer of various inspirational short stories and articles in print, resides in Eugene, Oregon.

"Long-Term Romance" by Ruth Bell Graham. From *It's My Turn* by Ruth Bell Graham. © 1982. Used by permission of Fleming H. Revell, a division of Baker Book House.

"Finding My Way Home" by Kay Marshall Strom. © 2001. Used by permission of the author.

"A Perfect Rose" by Melody Carlson from *Women Are Sisters at Heart* published by Countryman © 2000. Used by permission of the author.

"In a Hurry" by Gina Barrett Schlesinger. © 1996. Used by permission of the author. Gina Barrett Schlesinger dedicates this story to the memory of her mother, Alma Barrett.

"Special Delivery" by Richard Flanagan. © 2000. Used by permission of the author.

"The Gray Slipper" by Pearl Nelson, as told to Lynne M. Thompson. © 2001. Used by permission of the author. Lynne M. Thompson is wife to Pete, mother to Cassie and David, and a freelance writer from Modesto, California. Alberta Anderson passed away July 2, 2000. The gray slippers remain in Pearl's closet to this day.

"The Most Valuable Player" by Christine A. Redner. © 2001. Used by permission of the author.

"Precious Cargo" by Laurie Patterson. © 2000. Used by permission of the author.

SWEET MEMORIES

FAITH

"Streams in the Desert" by Kimber Annie Engstrom. © 2001. Used by permission of the author.

"The Breath of God" by Yitta Halberstam and Judith Leventhal. From *Small Miracles II.* © 1998. Used by permission.

"Animal Crackers" by Jennifer Tovell. © 2000. Used by permission of the author. You may contact her at 654 Harmony Road, Middletown, NJ 07748.

Quote by Charlotte Adelsperger © 2001. Used by permission of the author.

"Mom's Old Bible" by Jerry B. Jenkins from *The Story Jar* © 2001 by Multnomah Publishers. Used by permission of the author.

"The Twenty-Third Psalm for Women" by Judy Booth. From *Calm My Anxious Heart* by Linda Dillow. © 1998. Used by permission of NavPress. All rights reserved. For copies call 1-800-366-7788.

"May I Have This Dance?" by Nancy Jo Sullivan. From *Moments of Grace* by Nancy Jo Sullivan. © 2000. Used by permission of Multnomah Publishers, Inc.

"Blossoms of Kindness" by Betty Kehl. Reprinted from *Ripples of Joy.* © 2000 by Cheryl Kirking. Used by permission of WaterBrook Press, Colorado Springs, CO. All rights reserved.

"Snowflakes from Heaven" by Linda HoHonshelt. © 2001. Used by permission of the author.

"Road Map" by Barbara Darland. © 2001. Used by permission of the author. Barbara Darland is a popular conference speaker and former English professor at Multnomah Bible College in Portland, Oregon.

"The Christmas I Remember Most" by Robin Jones Gunn. Bestselling author of over forty-five books including *Mothering by Heart,* the Glenbrooke series by Multnomah Publishers, and the Christy Miller series. Used by permission of the author.

"The Greatest Question" by Anne Graham Lotz. From *Just Give Me Jesus* by Anne Graham Lotz. © 2000. Used by permission of Word Publishing, Nashville, TN. All rights reserved.

"Totally Awesome" by Charles R. Swindoll. From *Growing Deep in the Christian Life* by Charles R. Swindoll. © 1986, 1995 by Charles R. Swindoll, Inc. Used by permission of Zondervan Publishing House.